Another Cat at the Door

Books by C. W. Gusewelle

A Paris Notebook
An Africa Notebook
Quick as Shadows Passing
Far From Any Coast
A Great Current Running: The Lena River Expedition
The Rufus Chronicle: Another Autumn
A Buick in the Kitchen
On the Way to Other Country

Another Cat at the Door

BY

C.W. GUSEWELLE

EDITED BY

KATIE INGELS GUSEWELLE

THE LOWELL PRESS, INC. / KANSAS CITY

First Edition
Library of Congress Control Number: 2004113344

ISBN 0-932845-77-0

Illustrated by Tom Dolphens
Edited by Katie Ingels Gusewelle

Printed in the United States by
Greystone Graphics, Inc.

Published by
THE LOWELL PRESS, INC.
P.O. Box 411877
Kansas City, Missouri 64141-1877

DEDICATED TO

OLIVER	GRACE
OLIVER II	ALBERT
OLIVER III	KASHKA
ROOSEVELT	ZIPPER
SECRET	VALENTINE
FELIX	WALLY
ENA	LILA
ERIC	SCOOP
HEADLIGHT	TOMMY
SPANKY	STRIPE
TEDDY	MICKEY
SOPHIE	ELLIOT

AND TIP

INTRODUCTION

We were young then, my wife and I. What I brought to the marriage were three hunting dogs, two shotguns and an $800 debt to the IRS. She brought, besides the wonder of herself, a white cat whose name was Oliver.

I'd never lived with a cat before. And, though it dates me to say it, I'd never lived with a woman before. One of them I loved. The other one came in the bargain.

Perhaps because he was my first, he will always be, to my mind, the standard for all cats.

Oliver took the solemn measure of my dogs. Then he levitated over the back of a couch, like a missile bursting from its silo. And from that moment on they were his emotional slaves.

Almost before I knew it, he'd claimed my heart as well.

He was a significant cat of 18 pounds in his prime — affectionate, but also proud. He slept with his head between ours on the pillow, and in the moonlight through the window his profile was a lion's.

He was with us when our daughters were born, and was their first cat, too. The girls are grown now, and their careers have taken them to other cities. But never in all the years since have they been without cats.

They caught the fever from Oliver, and also, I suppose, from us. It was, my wife says, the one gene that passed intact.

We've had, among us, 24 cats since then — nearly all of them accidental. One jumped in our basket while we were picking apples. Another slipped into the garage through the dog door, and stayed ten years. Two were college cats. One came from a shelter for homeless men.

We're older now, and have come to terms with this hard rule: If you give your heart to these furred friends whose lives are short, there's sure to be sadness at the end. But the alternative is never to give your heart away at all — to anyone or anything. And what kind of choice is that?

Each of our cats has been different, each one prized. In some way, all of them are with us still — and will be always.

And these are their stories.

— C. W. Gusewelle

CONTENTS

THE EARLY TIMES

1. OLIVER

THE WHITE CAT, OLIVER, has had a good deal of trouble learning to speak.

His will to do it is not the problem. If an honest effort were all that counted, he would be reciting aloud from the classics and might already have a considerable reputation as an orator. But the art of plain talk has so far defied him.

He is, as I calculate, 9 years old, going on 10. But it is only in the last two years, or possibly three, that his fascination with the spoken word has been obvious.

My theory is that he just finally grew tired of the company of other cats. In some vague way he must recognize a kinship with them. But we all have had relatives who weren't much for visiting. And it's conversation he plainly wants.

What's more, he knows exactly what he wants to say.

He will enter a room, position himself in the center, wait for a lull in the talk, then — looking his listeners directly in the eye — say what's on his mind. Sometimes that amounts to an idle comment, and sometimes it's quite a lot.

He waits. And if there is no reply, he repeats himself. And if we still sit there mute as stones, he frowns and stalks away, pausing to turn and hurl back at us an irritable parting shot, a rebuke for our incivility.

This is not some exercise in cheap anthropomorphism, of the kind that ascribes wisdom to owls, nobility to lions or supernatural cunning to a fox. I have never believed that bear families live in woodland cottages and sit in clever little chairs and eat porridge.

A cat is a cat, nothing more. I am only reporting the observed and perfectly obvious fact that this one, the white cat, Oliver, is trying to talk.

His mastery of the consonant "r" is impressive. Delivered in an airy, offhanded way — a trilling *rrrrrrrrrrr!* with the inflection rising at the end — it is a greeting, a statement of his own well-being, an invitation to stroke him or even pick him up.

The same "r" has other uses. Preceded by a vowel, and spoken in a curt, peremptory way — *errr!* or *arrr!* — it denotes hunger and a desire for immediate service. The same syllable, swallowed and prolonged so that it resonates gutterally inside his chest, signals that he is vexed and wants his privacy respected.

Vowels in combination seem to confound him. On occasion he has been heard to utter a high-pitched *EEeeow*, plaintive and somehow metallic-sounding. One knows immediately, then, that he has either swallowed a hair ball or eaten too much grass and is about to throw up. But I have heard men make that sound in identical circumstances, have made it myself a time or two, and am not sure it qualifies as speech.

The dictionary defines speech as "the faculty of expressing thoughts by articulate sounds." This, I would argue, Oliver does, and in a fashion more pleasing than the tongue-clicks of certain aboriginal tribes.

What he says, he says plainly. But always in his language, never in mine. His vocal machinery limits him. And it is clear, if we are to pass very many satisfactory hours together discussing matters that interest us mutually — subjects more complex than hunger and hair balls and transient nausea — I must meet him halfway.

So I have undertaken the study of Felingua, the language of cats. And am able now to reproduce most of its identifiable sounds. Sitting in my chair, the two of us directly facing, I make a comment or two. And he corrects me. And, hearing the nuance that I had missed, I try it again. And yet again. Until I have gotten it right.

I repeat, it isn't foolish anthropomorphism that drives me. I am simply trying to do the polite thing by a cat who longs to talk.

Should I find myself one day in serious trouble with the law — homicide, pillage, antic indecency — I hope that my wife, if she happens to have a videotape of one of these sessions, will deliver it as evidence to the court. Based on the recent record of these enlightened times, it's safe to say no jury would vote to convict.

2 . F E L I X

FELIX, THE SPOTTED CAT, came to us a reject from friends — evicted for his kittenish habit of clawing his way up the screen of their porch. We're indiscriminate. We'll take the ones no one else will keep.

So playful as a youngster, he has gotten truculent in middle age. Some minor surgery recently required the shaving of one flank down to the skin. The fur is growing back, but slowly.

He is very vain, and his moth-eaten look has not improved his mood. Neither has the winter's long confinement.

Each morning, at the first sound of someone stirring in the house, he goes directly to the door and demands — does not just ask, *demands* — to be let out. If we do not oblige him nimbly enough, he is apt to withdraw into a sulk and give the rest of the day to planning retribution.

He is a comfort lover. In inclement weather the door scarcely interested him at all. But now, when the sun comes up warm and dew is on the grass and birds are singing, he claims a morning outing as his absolute right.

There is a dog on our street that has a reputation as a devourer of cats. Maybe it is undeserved, but the reputation follows him nonetheless. That one is the same dog that sits in the middle of the street, directly in the path of approaching cars. It's clear he doesn't give a damn about those machines. They can hit him or not — it's all the same to him.

The cars brake to a screeching halt. The dog eyes the motorist indifferently through the glass. Presently then, when it pleases him to, he gets to his feet with huge and languid disdain and removes his shaggy self just far enough to one side to permit the car to pass. Then he returns to his station in the street to test the next driver's nerve.

They met the other morning — that cat-eating, car-stopping dog and our misanthropic cat with the one ragged side.

The cat was sitting on the sidewalk in the sun. The dog was coming up the sidewalk toward his day's work at his favorite spot in the street. This crisis was observed from the window, and there was no time to intervene.

The dog marched steadily, deliberately forward, in the same way he has seen a thousand cars advance toward him. The cat remained sitting in place, expressionless, exactly as the dog does in the street. They examined one another levelly. Neither blinked.

I cannot help thinking that in that moment it occurred to them how much their natures were alike. And that those two stubborn, self-willed pedestrians of the morning recognized, each in the other, a kinship that transcended the mere accident of one of them being a dog, the other a cat.

It's the hour for my walk, the cat was plainly thinking. *And I'd advise you not to spoil it.*

And the dog, just as plainly: *Look, cats aren't on my agenda just now. I've got an appointment with some cars.*

For the duration of a held breath they were face to face, a foot apart. Then, not in friendship but in acknowledgement, they let their noses touch. And, each giving way slightly to one side, they passed on about their affairs in opposite directions.

Not all crises are negotiable, not all wars avoidable. But neither is diplomacy an invention of one species alone.

3 . ERIC

THE STARSHIP THAT WANDERS through space on a mission to seed the universe with cats has beamed down another alien onto our doorstep.

As Edgar Allan Poe is said to have cried, lying wretched in a gutter at the last: *Will it never end?*

We need more cats like Richard M. Nixon needed more tape recorders. We need cats like . . .

Never mind. You get the point.

This one is a tuxedo cat, with great galumphing

feet that suggest it could grow up to eat a dog. A minute after being discovered, the thing was in the house. Another minute or so and it was installed in a daughter's bedroom, already with a food dish, a bed and a litter box of its own. Before a strangled cry could rise in my throat, the discussion had every look of being already closed.

We canvassed the neighborhood by telephone. As soon as we stated our business, voices went chilly on the wire. Nobody knew anything at all about this beast. *Cats?* they asked. *What exactly are cats?* So I have posted a notice. People who advertise cats on office bulletin boards invite pity and ridicule. You'd do better offering used shoes and pre-owned underwear.

The telephoning and notice-posting are just perfunctory gestures, empty of meaning and without any hope of result. The cat is with us. I have been this way before, and I know how it always ends. So do the other creatures of our household.

The established cats — forgetting that they, too, were foundlings once — crouch outside the bedroom door, sniffing, making awful sounds in the back of their throats. They haven't yet seen the size of those feet. The time will come when they'll wish they'd been more cordial.

I try not to think about what's in the closed

room. I do not want to be told of the kitten's endearing antics. I'm pretending this hasn't happened to me, and that the note on the office board was put there by someone else. Already the cat has a name, Eric. Tomorrow, or the day after at the latest, he will have the run of the house and will be sending up coordinates to the mother ship so that another couple of dozen exactly like him can be transported down.

Twice before we gave found cats away to friends. And shortly afterward, both sets of friends left town without a word. Another time we took out an ad in the newspaper. The only response was a telephone call from a lecherous heavy-breather, who wanted to drop by sometime when I was likely to be away.

There is no use resisting destiny. I grumble, but I have learned — am learning, anyway — to sit back and take what luck brings. What it has brought most often, beginning with two beagles in my 20s and a cat or two a year since, is the promise of never being lonely when I sleep.

It could be worse. The starship could just as easily be sending down crocodiles and copperheads. Cats you can live with. Even a great many cats. Ask me. I know.

4. APRICOT CAT

ESTES PARK, COLO. — I JUST opened the cabin door and the cat was there. That's how it happens. Somehow, out of all the possible doors in the world, cats find their way to ours.

And he was a marvel, no doubt about it. Orange and white tiger-striped, with his tail handsomely ringed — the orange nearer a mellow apricot color. Fine, intelligent face. Sweet disposition.

Dear heaven, I thought, *not another one!* — and shut the door as quickly as I could. But I knew it wasn't any use. It's not blind chance that leads them to us. It's fate.

He stood outside, looking up at the door. And soon my wife observed him there and remarked on his uncommon excellence. And then my daughter — the one away at college, who had been speaking to us lately about the loneliness of her catless room.

A can of tuna fish was opened. Apricot cat ate his portion and, licking his whiskers, went away.

"He's somebody's pet," I said — the pitiful fiction of a man who's just seen his further destiny revealed. "Anyone can tell he's no stray."

But already the process was set in motion.

My wife spoke with the proprietors of the place. He'd been around for several days, they said. And, no, he wasn't a cat of anyone they knew. In a word, he was *available*.

"But see how smooth he is," I whined. "He's been taken care of."

"He was hungry," my ladies replied. The look in their eyes precluded argument.

Next a telephone call was placed to our daughter's landlord, who is making his quick fortune from the rental of student rooms. Yes, he said, the problem of catlessness could be corrected — but only at the price of a further cash deposit.

"How much?" we asked.

He named his figure — an amount that would make apricot cat a creature of value comparable to exotic beasts displayed in all the big international shows.

"The question is hypothetical," I told the man. "Maybe he won't come back."

But of course he did. That same day, and again the next. Persistence like that finally breaks you down.

"What you can do," I said to my daughter, "is leave your phone number. If no one claims him, the people here can call and you can come back for him." Her school was only an hour away.

But no sooner had I offered this surrender than the apricot cat disappeared. I watched for him — out of the corner of my eye, at first. Then I walked a bit around the grounds, thinking he might present himself. Finally, I stood at night outside the cabin door, an open tuna can in hand.

"What are you doing?" my daughter asked.

"What do you *think* I'm doing?" I said. "I'm calling the cat."

I don't know why that surprised her.

"Listen," I said, "he's an exceptional animal. A cat like that doesn't turn up every day."

"You sound upset."

"Let it be a lesson to you," I told her, a little testily. "Opportunity doesn't wait around. You take it when it comes, or you miss your chance."

5. SCANDAL

IT IS DISGRACEFUL, THE WAY we sleep. We've been away on a short trip, and our absence of a few days has worsened the shame of it.

Do not try to tell me that we were not missed. When we turned the car into the drive and opened the house door, the cats were waiting in a line, squinty-eyed with reproach. Our old dog, Cinnamon, another refugee from the streets and wonderfully sweet-natured, was just home from having her teeth cleaned. She followed us from room to room, grinning whitely.

A friend has given me a book, one chapter of which I try to read each night before retiring. Last night I put a page marker in the book and, as I got up from the chair and reached for the switch of the lamp, I looked for my wife in the bed.

I could not find her. The bed was covered with animals — two cats at the head of it, two more in the middle, the old dog sprawled across the bottom. Finally I spied my wife among them — just one of the tangle. And the years raced ahead in my mind to that time when the children will be gone and the insurance on me will have been collected and she will be alone in the house. But not alone, really. *Hardly alone!*

More cats and dogs will have come to lodge there. Through doors and windows left carelessly ajar they will wander in and out, unnamed and uninvited, bringing friends to stay the nights. She will mean to have them neutered — will fully intend to do that, but will forget. They will bear their careless litters in closets and behind the sofa and in the dark, untamed region of the basement.

The population will multiply ungovernably.

Strange tales will begin to circulate about the house and its thousand occupants. Neighborhood children, passing down the walk at night, will whisper among themselves and cross shuddering to the far side of the street.

Repairmen will refuse to answer calls there. The iceman will not cometh. The postman will not ring twice, or even once; he will apply for a change of routes. Meters will go unread and the lawn uncut. Neighbors will telephone the city with complaints.

She will, my wife, be like one of those fabulous crazed dowagers of the East — distant kin of a family of once-respected name but vanished means — dreaming away her last years in a cattery, surrounded by her trinkets and memories and by more love than is legal or sanitary.

Avant-garde cinematographers will come to document the amazing spectacle of ruin. But the film, though eloquent, will be deemed unfit for public viewing.

The presentiment of all this came powerfully to me as I searched her out last night among the varicolored heaps of fur on what, a long time ago, used to be exclusively our bed.

"The animals seem glad to have us back," I said. "But where's a place for me?"

She smiled a little smile from the edge of sleep.

The cats turned their green eyes upon me, level and defiant. The dog drew back her lips again and whitely grinned. And I returned to the chair to read another chapter in the book and wait my chance.

6. THE PREDATOR

SWOLLEN AMBITION IS an alarming thing to see. One morning last week Eric, the tuxedo cat, now fully ensconced in the house, appeared at the back door to display his catch. He was carrying a startled chipmunk by the nape of the neck, the way cats regularly transport their young.

He wanted to bring the prize inside. And when that wasn't allowed, he dropped it in dismay. The grateful chipmunk scurried away uninjured into its hole, and Eric sulked.

But the adventure has given him an altogether new estimate of himself.

The next day, from inside a window, he spotted bigger game. Flat against the sill, shoulders and haunches flexing in an imagined stalk, he watched a pilfering squirrel carry one of my tomatoes up a tree.

The day after that, it was a fat rabbit eating the flowers. Then the neighbor's Labrador retriever. And then the Monday trash truck. I'm gun-shy, now, about letting him out for his brief morning run, afraid he might find his way to the zoo and savage an elephant.

In other ways he's still a splendid cat. He is good with people. He tolerates being held and has never shown a claw. So even if he happened to be at large when one appeared, I do not seriously think he would drag down a meter man.

But at the beginning of every day, when the house is opened to let in the cool of that hour, he crouches just inside the door, staring fixedly at the wilderness beyond the screen. He knows there's more to life than being fed and petted.

Isn't that the restlessness in us all?

The merely pretty yearn to be ravishing. The moderately gifted hunger after genius. The man who only has a million covets a billion. The tin-pot politician dreams of being an emperor. The bankrupt republic wants to be a superpower. And now, in overweening vanity, a 14-pound cat imagines himself the master of the block.

"Go for it!" the indoor cats probably are saying, offering this advice from a safe distance in the rear. He's young still, Eric is, and doesn't know the lessons that time teaches. A lot of grief can come from overreaching. At least that's been my experience.

More cats have left this world through reckless arrogance than through humility, I tell him. But he doesn't listen — just waits at the screen, on the chance an undefended pit bull or careless Volkswagen might happen by.

7. ROOSEVELT

WE WERE PICKING APPLES in an orchard with our daughters when a tiny gray kitten appeared from between the trees and jumped in our basket.

"She's lost," said my wife. "I'll bet she needs a home."

A spell of dizziness came over me.

"Don't say that!" I groaned.

And we drove home with only apples, no cats. That night, though, just before bedtime, my wife spoke a memory of her girlhood.

"My father brought a gray kitten home in his pocket once," she said. And my fate lay clear before me.

The next day I drove an hour back to where we'd been picking, and the creature still was there. So I knocked at the house of the orchard's owners. Evidently she'd been abandoned, they said. Or maybe she was orphaned. At any rate, she'd just appeared one day at the end of the drive. And, yes, I'd be welcome to take her.

It is several days later, now — a sunlit morning in the bedroom. And as I write this the gray kitten is playing with an inflated balloon. She has a name, Roosevelt. That was the name the little girl so often heard spoken in the 1930s, and the name she gave to the one her father brought home.

I expect you know the nature of kittens — feisty,

inventive, unquenchably optimistic. The brilliance of autumn light falls in bars through the window, drawing sharp patterns on walls and floor. Past those and through them, large-eyed and untiring, Roosevelt pursues her pink balloon, pausing only to chew a catnip mouse, her other toy, or to investigate her tail.

But it is the balloon she prefers.

It is of respectable size for an adversary, but altogether helpless. It tumbles away foolishly when batted. The balloon has a painted face, a laughing one, that is about as large as Roosevelt's own. The laugh remains, even when the kitten snatches up the balloon near its stem and carries it with her teeth — though the eventual result of that is easy enough to guess.

She does not know the thing will sooner or later explode. Such an event is not in the limited range of her experience. Nor can she see, as I do, that inside the first balloon there is another, and inside that one perhaps another still. Not even I can see those faces, to know if they are laughing.

What Roosevelt cannot know, either — has no way of suspecting — is that within the hour she is to be put in a box and taken away to the veterinarian's for surgery. It will be an operation of the female sort, necessary if the cats of a household are not to increase their numbers exponentially.

All the same, this experience ahead will be her

first acquaintance with the unhappy fact of pain. Until now she has known nothing except food and fondling. This afternoon she will discover there is more — and worse. She will be baffled by it. To the extent that she is able to think in such terms, she may feel in some way betrayed.

I have been touched by this, watching her play here in the sun on the floor in the perfect trust of what is, in a sense, one of her last hours of kittenhood. Will she come back changed in ways never intended? Changed in heart? There is no helping that, I suppose.

But somehow, observing Roosevelt and her pink balloon, I cannot put out of mind the odd notion that I am seeing a metaphor for all our lives.

Gently it begins, or usually so. Life shows a laughing face. Then, like the balloon, it explodes unaccountably at our touch and reveals another face — endlessly, one face inside the other, some smiling and some not.

Perhaps a marriage ends, and in that unexplainable catastrophe a child's world is disassembled and rearranged. And so through all our years: careers blossom and then, in some moment, go wrong or are shunted in a new direction; a friendship ends, but another is gloriously made. Great losses and great gains.

And all of it — the good as well as the capricious

hurt — visited on us in a fashion we no more understand than the kitten, Roosevelt, understands the principle of balloons or the reason for the painful journey she is about to take.

Yet there happens a curious and touching thing.

Between these events it becomes possible to remember how to trust again. Never quite as freely, it is true. Never without a coin of caution in the shoe. But it does happen.

Kittens manage it, and so, almost always, do we. Being able to imagine our tomorrows requires it.

8 . A MID-LIFE CRISIS

THE WHITE CAT, OLIVER, has slipped off the edge and into his mid-life crisis. I have been there, so I know what he is going through.

Some of us announce the event by having nervous breakdowns. Others grow beards, or begin a sly affair. And some, like the stockbroker Paul Gauguin, give up job and family to answer the siren call of a different career.

These remedies are not available to a cat.

He has no way of knowing which of those other households along the street might greet him with a friendly hand, and which with a thrown shoe. He has grown accustomed to sleeping in upholstered chairs beside fires. He knows the exact placement of his food dish, and the sound of the can opener.

It is no use to remember the odd mouse caught or bird eaten over the years. Oh, Oliver is good, all right; he is talented in these matters. But a cat on the lam has to be good *every day*.

In a word, then, he is trapped.

There never is any telling exactly what triggers the mid-life collapse. In women it sometimes is said to be caused by the fading of beauty's bloom. In men, by the decline of sexual vigor — although the veterinarian some years ago removed that from the list of Oliver's concerns.

In his case, the crisis seems to have been provoked by the arrival in the house of the kitten, Roosevelt. Several previous additions to the menagerie he has endured sullenly, but without violent display. He bears, I think, no special malice toward this small newcomer. But sheer numbers have begun to tell on him. He has finally snapped.

The personality change has been dramatic and appalling. He has become a street brawler, a common thug.

It is a Jekyll-and-Hyde existence that he leads. He does not abuse the kitten. He frowns a lot, but does not attack. And when invited to, he still curls softly in a lap and purrs as winningly as ever.

But let a door stand ajar an instant and he is

through it and outdoors immediately, lip curled and spoiling for a fight. Somewhere, evidently, he has located another pugnacious cat.

I don't know how the other fellow looks, but Oliver comes home a wreck. His ears, which used to be so silky-pink, are cut and punctured and crusted now. There is a patch of fur gone from his forehead and an ugly welt across his nose. He looks the way George Plimpton, who wrote about his adventures as an amateur pitted against pro athletes, must have looked after three rounds in the boxing ring with Archie Moore.

This has been going on for days — no, weeks — now, and still they haven't settled it. Or maybe there is nothing to settle. I can't say about that other cat, but Oliver, I believe, is fighting just because it feels good. Feels better, at any rate, than simply sitting and staring out windows, brooding on the crisis that has overtaken him in his middle years.

I tell him that he'll burn himself out.

He comes reeling home at meal time all bloody and moth-eaten. And hunkers down scowling in front of his food dish. And gives the new kitten a long, even look as if to say, *You see what's happened, don't you? You see what's become of me, all on account of you?*

Then, after eating and sulking a while, he makes his way to my lap for consolation and advice.

"The thing is," I tell him, "you've got to pace yourself. You're burning the candle at both ends and in the middle, too. Keep on this way and you'll wind up just another punched out club fighter with funny eyes and headaches before you're 8."

Time is the great healer. One day, eventually, his rage will pass — it always does, with all of us. We accommodate to the changes in our lives and grow placid again. We shave off our beards and return to our spouses and ask for our old jobs back, deciding not to be painters — or, in Oliver's case, a mugger — after all.

It will happen, with patience.

But for now, he lays his tattered ears back flat against his head and leaves my lap with a growl. He already is planning the next battle. He is not quite ready yet to be told about coming to terms with his own limitations and the world as it is. And I understand.

Neither, for a long time, was I.

9 . EMPATHY

YOU HEAR IT SAID repeatedly — so often that it has acquired almost the cachet of fact — that our ability to feel empathy is one of the traits that sets our species apart from other, and by implication *lesser*, beasts.

That may be fine as theory. The trouble is that so much in actual experience argues against it. For example, I read in a magazine not long ago how wolves in the wild will feed and nurture an injured member of the pack until the hurt one has regained its strength.

All right, you say, but maybe that is not empathy at all, only self-interest. The wolf pack, after all, is a highly organized hunting unit. Isn't it possible the loss of one might lessen the chances for the others?

A fair argument.

But what about the story, circulated widely in the news, about that grizzly bear in Oregon and its friend, the cat? The 10-ounce orphaned kitten strayed into the pen at a wildlife rehabilitation center, where the bear had lived since being injured by a train. The 650-pound grizzly could have devoured the kitten in one bite.

Instead, he delicately selected a chicken wing from his lunch pail and placed it before the small visitor. From that moment, the two were chums. And what was in it for the bear, except perhaps relief from loneliness?

And there was the remarkable story out of Romania of an infant whose mother perished after being driven from the village by an anti-Gypsy mob. A nursing dog found the child by the path in the night, carried it to her den beneath a building under construction, and suckled it with her own pups. The child survived.

Such occurrences are only anecdotal, I suppose,

and prove nothing really.

But as I was considering them, I remembered a story even stranger and more wonderful that I once read, in *The New York Times* I believe it was, almost 30 years ago. It was a news item of only a few paragraphs on an inner page.

A yacht had gone down somewhere in a southern ocean, hundreds of miles from any land. The one survivor, a woman, swam until her strength was gone. Bereft of hope, she reconciled herself to death. Just as she was about to slip under, though, a great sea turtle rose up under her. In desperation, she grasped its shell.

For a day and a night — it may have been two nights — the creature swam on the surface of the sea. Finally a crewman of a passing freighter spied the woman. A boat was launched, and as rescuers lifted the woman half-delirious and gibbering to safety, they watched the great turtle glide away into the deeps.

Yet we, who are said to have a corner on empathy, will kill one another for a line on a map. Or for sport or for some trinket. Or kill one another on account of color, or ethnicity, or for holiness's sake.

To be famous for our compassion, and yet be capable of all that, must make us a most singular animal indeed.

10. FICKLE HEARTS

WE LOVE MOST INTENSELY that creature or that thing which we fear may soon be lost to us. The thing itself has not changed at all. But the imminence of its loss has made it priceless.

Consider the examples of snail darters and pupfish and the whooping crane.

It's likely that not one person in a thousand — or in 100,000 — had heard of the snail darter until a few years ago. Whole generations had gone to their graves without ever speaking its name, and so might ours have. Except that the damming of a certain river was proposed. The snail darter was found to live in that river and, worse yet, was determined to be rare. And as with all the other creatures we have driven to survival's edge, that small fish became immediately the object of fierce and quite widespread devotion.

Now the snail darter has entered into the popular vocabulary and become a part of our national consciousness. As the minnow goes, so goes public morality. If the snail darter perishes, ring down the long twilight of ruin.

In the same way, I have known people to drive several hundred miles round-trip on the chance — an outside chance at that — of seeing a whooping crane in the wild. And an authenticated report of a particular variety of pupfish observed gasping in some fetid desert puddle has been known to cause ecstasy of the sort usually inspired by the rose window in the Cathedral of Chartres.

Beauty is not the point. Probably the same passion would develop for cockroaches and dung beetles if there were known to be only seven of them left on earth.

But love is fickle. Let it be discovered that the snail darter is not endangered after all, that in fact there are whole river systems in which he teems in inestimable numbers, and our ardor for him will quickly cool. Let the whooping crane multiply beyond a certain point and you will hear him mentioned, if at all, only in terms of the fitness of his meat for the table.

All this is prologue.

A cat of ours became ill not long ago. The ailment wasn't serious but we did not know that at the time. The symptoms were ominous.

Now this particular cat had a bad habit or two. Never mind just what those were — suffice that they were bad. But with the onset of the illness, it was amazing how these faults of his were brushed aside by our sudden new appreciation of his general excellence.

He became, for several days, the central figure in our household. He was endlessly held and comforted and stroked. His name was being spoken constantly and his virtues recited. He could do no wrong. There even was talk of letting him outdoors.

In due course he was examined. The results were inconclusive, and our concern mounted. He was taken to another city for tests of a more elaborate and more expensive sort. By this time cost did not matter, so great was his surpassing fineness as a cat.

Then the news was received, along with the bill.

The news was that he was not sick at all. Never had been. The symptom that so alarmed us had been just one of those things that happens from time to time with cats — a minor indisposition that has, and needs, no explanation.

You would not believe the change of attitudes. He must wonder again why his name is so rarely spoken, except when linked with a curse at his old habits. If he mews at the crack of the door, a shoe toe moves him brusquely, and pitilessly, aside. He is just a cat again. A cat that cost a lot.

His symptoms have disappeared entirely. Gone, too, is any memory of the lesson we might have learned. We have become indifferent and unforgiving again.

That's how it goes with snail darters and cats and all the other things and creatures in our lives — even the people in them — when we imagine they will last forever.

1 1 . COMFORT LOVERS

IN A SUDDEN BLAST OF wind and pelting rain, the season turned. But because it happened in the afternoon, and they are mostly indoor cats with only a few morning minutes for exploring in the yard, the change took them by surprise.

Eagerly, that next dawn, they crowded at the door. Gladly they charged forth — and halted in mid-step, turning their astonished faces back, eyes fixed with regret on the door as it closed behind them.

What's this? their expressions plainly said. *Who cancelled sunrise? Where'd the easy days go?*

There's no use looking for mouse or chipmunk on such a morning. Any creeping thing with a burrow has sense enough to stay bedded in it. Frosted grass is no good for eating, and worse for rolling in. All the good things were subtracted overnight.

Minutes later they were back — the white one on the step, peering through the glass door with a worried look; the black one hunkered on an old iron stove from which no memory of warmth issued. Inside, they knew, were food bowls and radiator tops. Inside, their names would be spoken.

It's pitiful to get tamed that way, but time and a little comfort can do it to us all.

I can't say how many past mornings I've wakened in a

hunting camp with a crackling sheath of ice frozen on my sleeping bag. It used to be I could kick the snow aside and build a cheering fire, and roll up in a tarpaulin directly on the iron ground, without even a tent. Immediately, it seemed, the blue morning would start to come and it would be time to poke the embers and set the coffee on.

I remember those times as if they were something I'd only been told about, or that happened a long time ago to a stranger.

To do that now would be, at best, an unbearable misery, at worst, fatal. The difference between adventure and foolishness has gotten clearer. If the outside temperature drops much below 65 degrees, I want to hear a furnace throbbing nearby. If there's a bed, I want to sleep in it. If there's a magnificent snowfall, I prefer seeing pictures of it in a magazine.

My idea of roughing it is to ride in late November in a car with a weak heater.

We used to be creatures in nature, the cats and I. Then we found homes, and gentle hands, and developed effete habits, like eating things we didn't have to chase and catch. And as will happen, we became prisoners of our ease.

It's a splendid condition, I thought. And opening the door, I let them come shouldering back inside to the soft chair they plan on occupying until wild geese and baseball players head north again in spring.

1 2 . SECRET CAT

THE OLD CAT SLEEPS BESIDE the telephone and has never had a call. Has never had a friend.

She was a lady of the streets for as long as age was on her side. But she waddles now. Her tattered hair skirts drag the snow. Her beauty mark, a notched ear, is wasted on the prowling toms.

I'll never forget how she came to us, through a dog door into the garage during a nasty spell of weather. At about that same time, there was a story in the newspaper about a man who'd shot his mother-in-law in his garage, explaining he'd mistaken her for a raccoon.

It was lucky I wasn't armed when the old cat arrived. Secret Cat, we've named her, because when we brought her in the house she hid herself somewhere in the basement for most of a fortnight, only coming out to empty the food bowls we kept filled and to use the litter box we provided.

Other cats have come and gone — undone by years or by the wheels of some indifferent car. The old cat stays, cautious and durable, nested safely now amid the clutter of books and papers on the telephone table, from which, with slitted eye, she observes life passing. None in all that procession of other creatures has cared much for her.

The dog waits for her around the corner of the

stair. The cats, allies of the dog for purposes of ambush, crouch atop and under and behind the furniture. Returning from some small excursion, the old cat — the friendless one — peers into the darkness of the open doorway and considers the gantlet to be run, measures the distance to her perch. Then makes a dash for it.

Out the others come then, erupting from the shadows in hot pursuit. It's all for sport. They've never caught her and do not mean to catch her. They only want to humiliate her by causing her to scurry and scramble.

Something about her must invite torment. Does her manner betray the insecurity, the shame, of having once been a winter stray? Whatever the reason, her entries are all the same, all noisy and harried. Even the smallest, clumsiest kitten new to the household soon joins the baying rabble at her heels.

She has perfected the art of being inconspicuous. If it were not for our using the telephone, we might forget she lived with us at all. She sleeps a lot, as old cats do. When stroked, or scratched behind an ear, she seems surprised and a bit uneasy. She objects to being held.

One could almost suppose that she had achieved so final a state of wariness or disillusionment that affection no longer figured in her plans. And yet . . .

Twice in these years there have been periods

when, through some sequence of sad misfortune, the old cat was the only creature remaining to us. The losses left empty places in our house and in our hearts — deficits which the strange, shaggy, reticent survivor moved promptly to rectify.

She left her station beside the phone and found the courage to strop herself against a trouser leg. At night she curled at the foot of the bed where one or more of the others had previously slept.

It was not so much that her nature had changed. The caution still was there. After having passed so many solitary hours she had no sense of how to be a lap cat, nor do I think she wanted to be. Her purpose in those times seemed to be less in receiving attention than in giving it. It was as if, responding to our need, she played the pet as best her misshapen temperament would let her.

After several weeks, then, the replacement cats would begin to arrive. And immediately — though with no show of pique or resentment — the old girl would return to her accustomed habits, taking up her place beside the phone again, waiting for that call that never comes. And soon the new cats would learn to devil her and lurk beside the door.

These other ones I value for their glossiness or grace or other virtues. The old cat I value for the goodness of her heart.

I remember those times when she was not just kept — when she was *needed*. And I am led to think that there must be a great deal of unknown and unsuspected tenderness about, like the consideration in that old cat, waiting only for space and reason to be noticed.

1 3 . P O O R T O L S T O Y

ERIC, TUXEDO CAT, HAVING just savaged the ribbon of the typewriter and made any further writing impossible, was sitting atop the machine, pleased with his work.

"Look at him," said my wife. "Do you know where that cat belongs?"

"In the oven?" I replied.

"That's an awful thing to say. He belongs on a book jacket. Every writer worth anything has his picture taken with a cat."

"Tolstoy despised cats."

"How do you know that?"

"Have you ever seen a picture of him with a cat?"

"I don't know that I've seen his picture at all."

"Well, look in the encyclopedia," I told her. "You won't see any cat in the picture of Tolstoy."

"He didn't even have a typewriter," said my wife. "I'm talking about modern writers. Go in any book store and see for yourself."

"It's a silly convention. Those aren't live cats anyway."

"What do you mean, not *live?*"

"There is a taxidermist in the East Village in New York who rents out stuffed cats to the big publishing houses to use in picture of their authors."

"But I've seen TV interviews where the cats moved."

"Battery-operated," I told her. "When the interview is finished they're boxed up and taken back to the taxidermist."

"Why would anyone do that?"

"It's the literary business," I said. "If people want scandal and gossip, that's what publishers give them. If they want sex, they give them sex. If they want cats, they get cats. Anyway, it's less trouble with the stuffed ones."

"In what way?"

"They don't eat. They don't need a litter box. They don't rip the ribbons out of typewriters. All you have do is dust them now and then, and rub a little oil in the fur to keep them shiny."

"What you say may be true," she said. "But I still think Eric looks wonderful sitting there. Every typewriter needs a cat."

"Listen," I told her, "I make my living with that machine. If he's going to hang around my desk, he has to behave."

"Eric is very trainable," she said.

And that's when I got the idea.

"Do you think he could be trained to write?"

"Maybe," she said. "Remember how he used to play the piano at night. Somehow, though, I don't see him as a novelist."

"No, but he might be able to do simple stuff."

"Like columns?" she said.

"Why not? If he could just do one occasionally it would take some of the pressure off."

"I don't know," she said. "Cats are awfully independent. What about that nice high school boy you had lined up to do it?"

"He said he didn't want to fool with writing. He's going to mow lawns instead."

"That's a pity."

"Yes," I said, "ambition is unattractive in the young."

"So what will you do?" she asked.

"I'm going to start by getting the cat off the typewriter and getting a new ribbon."

"And then?"

"Then we'll see."

"Can he be on the next book cover?"

"We can talk to the printer," I told her. "But I don't think cats hold up so well going through the press."

14. KEPT BEASTS

A T FIRST LIGHT THEY ARE waiting on the wire, huddled small inside their feathers, eyes fixed on the door. Jay and sparrow, junco and cardinal, ungainly starling — all made beggars by the snow and by their hunger.

In men or birds, hunger is the great leveler.

From the wire, from the rail of the fence and from their perch in a low, leafless bush, they will watch the door an hour. If it opens, and the woman comes out with a can of seed, they will hurry to be saved. If she forgets, or is gone away somewhere, they will flutter coldly on to other houses, other doors.

And if all the doors remain shut, if no one appears to feed them and the snow and cold last, they will perish. A country bird has wider opportunities. But a city bird is charity's prisoner, hostage to a will beyond its own.

Inside the windows of the house are the cats, looking out. The same woman who feeds the birds also keeps cats. The cats watch the birds, and the birds, between their peckings at the seed, watch the cats looking at them.

The cats are mostly indoor cats, and have never caught a bird. They know birds only through the glass. But they know the *uses* of birds, just as birds know the *intentions* of cats. What neither knows is how alike their situations are.

Because the cats' food bowls at that early hour also are empty of food. If the woman, after coming in from the birds, should forget the cats, hunger would begin to gnaw.

The barn cat, like the country bird, can improvise. He can prowl the hayloft for a nest of mice, or hunt the road ditches in the frozen dark. He might ache from bedding in cold places, or wear ragged ears from disputes with other ruffians of his kind. But he survives by his wit, and he knows the holes where supper lives.

The house cat is a mendicant. Maybe there is a mouse in the basement, and maybe not. If there is, maybe some old memory will remind him how to catch it. And after that one mouse, what?

The house cat looks through the glass at the woman as she feeds the birds. Then he looks at his own empty bowl. And at the other cats, looking at *their* empty bowls. What if the house should be silent for a long time? What if footsteps were to cease, and the rattle of the food box were not to be heard again? Ever.

A humiliating anxiety fills them all.

The woman never forgets. Until now, at least, she never has. But that's the danger of being a dependent thing, a *kept* thing — whether you're a bird trained to the feeder, or a house cat trained to the hum of the electric can opener. Or a wage worker, trained by a lifetime's habit in some other man's employ.

Everything has its price. And the price of the comfort of letting yourself be kept is, in the end, an awful insecurity. I think of that whenever I read of some company failing, and its people being flung out unwarned and unprepared into the jobless cold.

And in those times I envy the country bird and the barn cat, hunting the tunnels of the high grass, plucking the wild seed, taking their chances — owing nothing and expecting nothing, living by an art that, past a certain age, is hard to learn.

15 . A BORROWED ROOM

FULTON, MO. — THE HOUSE in which I am lodging now, a guest, has emptied of its racket and confusion of several years ago. The sons have grown and gone. And the rooms from which one or another of them used to be displaced to make way for visitors are untenanted now.

Not empty, mind you. Just not regularly lived in anymore. The rooms still are their own. Their books remain on the shelves — some of them, at any rate. Their saved articles from the various stages of boyhood still are to be seen on the walls and desks and on the fine old carved ledges above the doors.

These leavings are not preserved morbidly, as shrines. It is just that 20 years and more of occupancy make durable marks. If nothing else, nail holes in the wall must be kept covered. And what better way to cover them than to let hung things stay in their place?

So, if the boys ever were to come back here to live — back from Africa or the far west or the north country or the other side of town, wherever their luck has taken them — they would find the evidence of themselves remaining. In the natural way of growing up and growing away, however, that is unlikely to happen. Or, if it happens at all, not for long.

My friends, their parents, pretend to be untroubled by the stillness. Their own lives race foward, creative, occupied with ideas and values and the untiring defense of sense in a world tending ever toward senselessness. Or maybe they are not pretending, for they are realists. They grew up and went away themselves. They know it happens.

Even so, I have to think that sometimes, in the quiet of the evening, they must look up from a book or the stack of papers to be graded and listen for a footstep on the stair. Or, in passing the open door of one of these upstairs rooms, that they might, just for an unguarded instant, find it odd to see the bed unslept-in. They don't speak about that, though.

One of humanity's virtues is the ability to come to terms with change.

With other creatures it's different. With a cat, for instance.

Today, with this bit of writing to do, I turned on the lamp in one of the unoccupied upper rooms and arranged myself and my working things at the borrowed desk. Above the door at the left were two footballs. On the bookcase behind, a model ship. On the table at the right, some arcane mechanical construction and also an empty Irish beer bottle. On the desk's top was a wind-up alarm clock with its spring run down. And in the desk drawers were — among many other things — a box of broken crayons, a fuzzless tennis ball, assorted small bicycle parts and a folder marked *"Personal Letters,"* into which I had the decency not to pry.

Having oriented myself by these investigations, I began to work. But before very long I sensed a presence near at hand. It was the cat of the house, sitting in the doorway, sizing up the situation with cool green eyes.

The meaning of what followed could not have been plainer if the cat had suddenly been empowered to speak her thoughts aloud.

By her puzzled expression, it was obvious the look of me sitting there at the desk was somehow slightly wrong. And possibly the smell of me as well. Yet, at the same time, she found it good to see the room again in use — the lamp burning, the chair sat in, and one of those man animals busy with his incomprehensible occupations.

So she rose, the cat did, and came a bit uncertainly across the threshold.

I put down my hand and she examined it, and slightly shied away. It was not the proper hand. But then she relented and let herself be stroked. The foot and leg, too, were somehow wrong. She turned those green eyes up directly into my own with a speculative look.

Who the hell are you? she demanded to know. *You're not the one who used to sit there — who ought to be sitting there again.*

But then she appeared to have an afterthought. Better an old boy than no boy at all, her manner seemed to say. Anyway, a room needs to be lived in. The lamp shone warmly. The clutter of papers and the click of the typewriter were reassuring.

So she flung herself against my trouser leg, and rubbed there companionably. And then, quite satisfied, demanded to be let outside to explore the winter yard.

I will be sorry for her sake — for her sake only — to gather up my things one day shortly and leave the room to silence and her memories again. Cats, contrary to their reputation, can't lock their hurts behind a poker face.

If you imagine otherwise, you don't know cats. Or losses.

16. THE WHISPERER

HE WAS AN EXCEPTIONAL cat. Even sprawled in a busy intersection, stunned by the wheel or bumper of a car, his excellence was apparent.

In another minute or so, however, he was apt to be a good deal flatter and less exceptional. So my wife, who has a sharp eye for livestock, collected him from the street and brought him home.

That's how they've come to us, all but one of them, by some accident or other. Except for the law and the neighbors, there's no upper limit on the number we would keep. The resident cats demonstrate for a day or two, then move aside and make room. The household stabilizes again. And we settle back to await the next accident, the next cat.

This one was no alley cat, though. After the trauma of the street had passed, he was wonderfully gentle. What's more, there'd been some financial investment in him, of the kind you make when you like cats but think their numbers ought to be finite.

So someone had cared about him. And someone

might be missing him.

We advertised in the classified columns. The ad generated an obscene call. We were charmed that anyone would organize his day's lascivious whisperings around the lost-animal ads in the newspaper. There is a case for neutering, all right, and not just of cats.

There also were two or three legitimate calls, in which people described their lost cats and we described the one we had. Always he was the wrong cat. The callers sounded a bit put out that we had advertised, but probably they were only disappointed.

By this time, several days had passed and the cat was still in the back room, still apart from the others who knew that he was there but pretended not to notice. And we had accustomed ourselves to the idea that we might not keep him, after all.

Not wanting to excite the whisperer with another classified ad, I put a notice on the office bulletin board. Some strange people work there, and what they say over the telephone is their own affair. But at least, I thought, the offer of a cat would not inflame them to lewdity.

I was wrong. Some of their comments, on reading the notice about the cat, were very coarse indeed. Most just ignored it. I enlarged on the note, restating the offer in language a bit more florid.

And I discovered a principle. If you ever want to

know a lot about your colleagues — their allergies, the cramped size of their apartments and so forth — just put up a note about a cat. They'll tell you everything. Everyone has an excuse, and the excuses range from new Oriental carpets to killer parakeets.

Not to prolong the suspense, an associate at the office did finally take the creature. Or rather, his mother did. She happened to be visiting from several hundred miles away. But he persuaded her to have a look and, like my wife, she is a fine judge of catflesh.

Her previous cat had been fed a daily ration of liver and yeast and had lived 27 years before dying in her lap. Our lodger rode away with her in the car, to a home on a shady street in a quiet town, not even beginning to suspect yet what a deal he had fallen into.

So, to the posted notice, I added a bulletin saying the cat was gone. Immediately people began coming out of the office woodwork — a lot of them.

I knew someone who wanted that cat of yours, they said. Or, *He sounded like a hell of a cat, that one did.* Or, *I'd made up my mind to take him. I was going to tell you in about an hour.*

Their expressions were heavy with disappointment and reproach.

Thus was revealed a second principle: If you ever want to know the intensity of your friends' devotion to cats, just let it be known discreetly that they've missed their chance.

1 7 . EQUILIBRIUM

PUT ENOUGH CREATURES under one roof — two-legged, four-legged, smooth-skinned and furred, all sharing the same space, the same beds, the same parasites and occasionally the same food — and the equilibrium gets fairly delicate.

But such a household, if that's what it can be called, is not assembled overnight. It happens insidiously, like the growth of the national debt. So that before the crisis is noticed, it already is past any hope of remedy.

The catastrophe begins modestly enough.

Two innocents stand before a minister and their lives are joined. The cat of one of them, and the dogs of the other, also are joined — noisily at first, but joined.

And why not? Who would want to pass through lonely years and on into great age, bitter in the memory of a love fumbled away because of one Persian shorthair and two arthritic beagles?

Children come. A larger house is needed. The cat expires, and afterward the beagles. The rooms seem empty without them, the family diminished. Replacements must be quickly found. But after that another cat appears on the lawn. And yet another, orphaned in an orchard, clambers into the basket of apples.

All the rest move over to make room.

A winter storm drives a homeless hound to shelter on the step. Friends get a kitten, but find it neurotic and destructive. The painlessness of euthanasia is slyly mentioned. The others move over again, and that one brings to the mix his Prussian name, Felix, and his crazy inclinations.

Still, the man of the place is troubled at times by a sense of something lacking. What might it be? The man is a hunter. The cats are hunters, too, and gifted ones. But the game they wait for at a crevice in the basement wall is nothing fit for table. And cats do not point birds.

So what the man needs is a bird dog. He gives it as an early birthday present to himself, and gives the present a name, Rufus. The new pup's arrival inspires a lively yowling as the deck is reshuffled yet again.

In time, the house comes to seem smaller. Privacy is rare, loneliness impossible. One reaches for one's sandwich on the plate and finds it gone. A roast put out for thawing disappears. Blame cannot be assigned. The many eyes follow you guiltlessly, awaiting your next mistake.

I have been deliberately imprecise here about actual numbers. The law is meddlesome in that regard, and there is no point alarming the neighbors.

Some years ago a friend journeyed from a far city

to stay the night with us. He made the mistake of leaving his bedroom door ajar, and appeared at breakfast haggard and amazed. It was, he said, like sleeping in Kruger National Park. He has been back once or twice since. But always with only enough time between planes to meet for a restaurant meal.

For the moment, now, we are in equilibrium. The numbers are stable. But I am overtaken sometimes by the knowledge that, out there in the jungle of the streets, cats and dogs are multiplying tirelessly, and that in the inevitable course of things some of the results of those dalliances will find their way to us.

We are not just cranks. We are part of a vast and majestic process. And who can guess its end?

18 . THE JUNGLE HOUR

THE RAW SHANK OF WINTER has given way to spring. The weather has softened. Morning is the jungle time, and life has gotten more complicated.

Through the back door and into the early light they come rushing all together, trying to remember the wild things they used to be. It must be an electric moment for the smaller wildlife of the yard.

The tuxedo cat, Eric, goes directly for the dark tangle of bushes beside the fence, vanishing in the shadow. The bird dog stylishly points a tree in whose higher reaches he has spied an impudent squirrel. The white cat, after rolling in the dust, imagines himself camouflaged and settles in plain view to wait for a feeble-minded chipmunk.

The squirrel is sure-footed. He peers down bright-eyed from his branch. The chipmunk watches safely from his hole, knowing a dirty white cat is no more trustworthy than a clean one. Birds long ago gave up nesting above a yard in which upturned green stares awaited the fledgling generation.

Meantime, the gray cat has climbed a tree to the garage roof, explored to a corner of the eave and then forgotten the way back. She sets up a pitiful wailing. So I have to get the ladder and fetch her down.

As I'm dealing with the ladder and the cat on the roof, Eric goes over the fence, his leap cushioned by my tomato vines, and goes around to hide himself under a bush by the front step. He enjoys the sound of his name called in tones of growing concern. It would humiliate him to come when summoned. He prefers to materialize, owlishly, when the seeker's back is turned.

By now it's getting on in the morning. The sun is far above the trees. The early haze is gone, and the jungle is just a yard again. The cats are thinking of cozy rooms, of cushions, of the day's activity in the kitchen and the lucky accidents that sometimes flow from that. After their quarter-hour of liberty, they gladly come in.

I'm ready for my ration of oatmeal and a rest, and to try to salvage what's left of my day. But I still must find where the bird dog, Rufus, has buried his food dish and inspect the fence perimeter to see how many new escape tunnels he's begun.

This is not the shape I imagined life would take in these years.

Magazines with names like *Gracious Living* and *Modern Maturity* show couples taking slow breakfast at outdoor tables, smelling the flowers, smiling happily together as they read the stock market quotations. Their children, if they have them, already are grown and living in apartments or houses of their own, have made big successes and regularly surprise Mom and Dad with little gifts of airline tickets to Europe or Hawaii.

If the magazine couple has a pet, it is a golden retriever that lies tranquil at their feet — a dog that neither barks, harbors fleas, poaches at the cats' pans nor excavates, and may in fact be a stuffed animal — so that when they go off on their frequent holidays the kennel bill does not exceed the cost of the trip itself.

I envy the picture-book life, even as I find its sterility somehow terrifying. In the photograph there is no cat on the garage roof. What does that man do with all his time? I doubt if he even owns a ladder.

19. TIME FOR CARING

THERE IS, AMONG THE creatures we patronizingly call "dumb," a surprising amount of understanding. Call it only intuition, if you like. But, by whatever name, the display of it sometimes is amazing.

The white cat, Oliver III, met misfortune the other day and came home groggy and disabled. For that day and several afterward, he was a deplorable case, unable to stand and walk or even, at first, to raise his head.

We installed him in the bedroom on a pallet of towels with a cover over him for warmth. From his nest, he peered out helplessly, eyes lusterless and confused.

Evening came, the hour when Rufus is brought in from his fenced backyard run to enjoy the touch of hands and take his greater ease in upholstered chairs. He's a rowdy, that pup. Sly thief of food from the old dog's bowl — the same food as his own, but tastier for being stolen. And a joyous bedeviler of cats.

Now Oliver, in the fullness of his powers is nothing to be trifled with. The sound that issues from his chest when he's annoyed can turn a challenger's blood to ice. But that's when he's himself. The pitiful thing in the towel bundle was perfectly defenseless.

So how would the others respond? Would they take it as a time for settling accounts? And how about the bird dog, especially? He bore no grudges that we knew of. But his one gait is an incorrigible romp, badly suited to a sickroom.

We took the chance, though, and let him in.

One bound inside the bedroom door and he stopped. Just stopped stock-still, then sat — nose thrust slightly forward to identify the patient, his face (for animals' features can be wonderfully expressive) mystified and grave.

Sitting there, the pup raised one forepaw as if to playfully box. There was no motion from the bundle. The glazed eyes remained slitted nearly shut. The paw was lowered and the dog sat a moment longer, considering.

You have read, perhaps, how elephants will stay with a stricken member of the herd and, even after death, will use their trunks to try to urge the fallen individual to regain its feet and continue on the march.

Well, that's just what the dog did next. He drew close on soft pads, reached out his nose and, with a gentleness quite uncommon for him, administered several little nudges that said, plain as anything, *Get up. It's wrong to see you lying there so still. I'll bet you can get up if you'll only try.*

At the moment, though, the white cat was beyond any such effort. He just drifted in his daze, and gave no sign. Whereupon the dog lay down exactly beside him, parallel and very near, but with face turned a bit sideways so that he could notice any stirring. At that moment, for whatever reason, he preferred that place on the floor to the softness of his usual chair.

My wife came up from downstairs, then, and reported the strange behavior of the other cats. Like most of their kind, they're individuals and not much on collaboration. They keep a civil distance, although that's not how she had just found them.

"They're all sitting on the hall carpet," she said. "Close together in a kind of circle as if they'd been talking it over."

It can get crowded sharing a house with so many others of such different wants and shapes. Crowded, and sometimes inconvenient. But two legs or four, clever or dumb, we're there for one another when caring's of any use.

2 0 . T E L E P A T H Y

THE CATS HAVE PSYCHIC powers. There is no other explanation.

One evening last week, my wife took two cans of tuna from the cupboard and placed them on the kitchen work table, planning to make a tuna salad the next day.

From earliest kittenhood, the cats of our household have been alert to the sound of the electric can opener. For them, as for me, it is the announcement of happiness forthcoming.

That little mechanical growl calls them from whatever they are doing to arrange themselves in an expectant line on the counter by the telephone.

As I've said, though, she didn't open the cans that evening. Just got them out, and then retired. The next day, an invitation to lunch or some other glamorous alternative to tuna presented itself. So it was yet another day before the canned fish came into play.

For sanitation's sake, the electric opener is partly disassembled after each use, the components washed separately and stored in a drawer. That is the same drawer that holds knives, spatulas, the tea strainer, old wine corks, salad tongs, and an assortment of unmatched spoons. We probably open it 15 or 20 times a day, without evoking the least excitement.

Well, my wife went in the kitchen and opened the drawer — this being, now, the morning after the day after the evening when the cans first appeared. She could have been getting a spoon to stir her coffee. She could have been doing any of a hundred things in that drawer, but, in fact, she was getting out the parts of the can opener.

Had not actually laid hands on them, you understand. Was only *preparing* to. When, looking up, she saw that row of round faces, transfixed with lust, watching from the accustomed place at the counter's edge.

They were there already.

"It can't be true," I said when she told me about it. "You must have made some sign."

"No. They just knew."

"I don't like it," I said, and gave a little shiver.

"Don't like what?"

"It's not natural."

"Why not? You always know when the hot doughnuts come out of the cooker, and the doughnut shop is 40 blocks away."

"That's normal instinct," I told her. "But this is weird. Where are they now?"

"They're all lying upside-down on the windowsills, sunning themselves."

I noisily opened and closed the drawer beside the kitchen counter.

"What are they doing now?"

"They're still in the windows," she said. "They know you're not serious."

"So you see, it was just a coincidence."

"You don't understand cats," she said, and wrote something on her notepad beside the phone. "You don't understand cats at all."

She'd printed it in big block letters on the pad: T-U-N-A.

Then *she* opened the drawer.

And I do not think you would be altogether comfortable knowing what happened next.

21. SHARED GRIEFS

"I'M AFRAID WE'RE losing him," she said.

And I told her, "No, he'll be all right, believe me." Because I wanted more than anything for that to be true.

She was right, though, and I was wrong. The veterinarian called, and in a gentle voice — because the veterinarian also is a friend — he said, "I was holding him at the end. There's nothing else we could have done."

And in those few words, the great white cat, Oliver, passed from our lives, taking a bit of all of us with him.

I don't mean to make too much of this. Life is composed in the half part, at least, of losses. And we have friends whose losses have been so terrible as not even to be decently mentioned in the same breath as this one of ours.

What's more, in remembering him, there's no use idealizing. He had his faults — was vain and pugnacious in his younger years, grew crotchety and demanding as he aged. But he also could be wonderfully tender when it suited him. And toward the last, it suited him more and more.

He had a way of insinuating himself under an arm or onto the bed beside you as you slept. He had fine, intelligent eyes and a large, regal head. He looked directly at you when he spoke, and, with patience, he taught us a few of his words.

He was our children's first cat, and lasted until they are now about to leave. Oliver and the old dog were young together. They slept pressed side by side, and washed each other's ears. Then more cats came, and after those a rowdy pup, and always he accommodated. Each time he was the one who offered peace. It's what you can do if you're confident of your place.

We discussed it briefly. I'm not much for burying in a cold, wet yard. So he's gone to ashes, and when the ground warms we'll put those beside a tree he liked to scratch, and we'll plant a flower there.

I went to the veterinarian's place for a last visit in the privacy of one of the small examining rooms. He was so little changed. I took his ear between my fingers and felt the familiar little bump that was a healed scar of antique battle. I touched his whiskers that, brushing at my face, so often tickled me awake. His fur was soft under my hand.

It helped to do that, though I'm glad there was no

one there to watch.

That evening we talked, and shared our pain in remembering. We toasted, with raised glasses, the wonder of a cat he'd been. And it seemed we might muddle on more or less all right from there. But in a small hour of night, the door opened and the brightness from the hall fell suddenly on our bed. It was one of our daughters, standing there against the light.

"It's Cinnamon," she said, her voice broken. *"She's going from room to room. She can hardly see, but she's trying to find him."* In our selfish sadness, we'd forgotten about the old dog.

We listened, then. And we could hear her — pacing tirelessly from one corner of the house to the other, her nails clicking on the wood of the floors below, understanding nothing, perhaps, though sensing everything, half-blinded by cataracts but hunting, hunting with her nose for the nearness of her friend, the cat of all her years.

Grief is grief. Even in its humbler forms it's sometimes damned near insupportable.

THE MIDDLE TIMES

22. TEDDY

A FILL-IN WAS ALL HE WAS, a substitute white cat to occupy the space left suddenly in a house that was used to having one.

"He's white, is he?" we asked. "We'll take him, then." Aside from the color, we weren't particular. A cat like the one we'd lost you don't replace. You just try to plug the hole with something white.

So the new one arrived, fresh from a country brawl. He'd been a drifter, and after that a barn cat, the folks who brought him said — shunted from place to place. And he would take no prize for looks. His coat, though white as promised, was coarse and rough. His face, swollen on one side, was cut and crusted from the latest encounter.

The other cats of the house took one look at the battered thug and began to sing their cat song of terror and indignation. He looked at them out of his good eye, the other mattered nearly shut. He was unimpressed by their singing. He didn't retreat — just fixed them with that level one-eyed stare that seemed to say, "It's your move. But I'm warning you, I've been worked over by experts."

We had a sudden vision of weeks, possibly years, spent refereeing cat disputes.

"Maybe we won't keep him," we said. "We might

have to get rid of him." Though finding a home for anything that looked like that would not be easy.

We confined him a week in the upstairs bedroom. The other cats came to sing their rage under the closed door. He healed, looked more presentable. And feeling better, he emerged and claimed a chair.

The previous white cat, Oliver, had been the third in a line of kings. But this one was a peasant. We tried the old name a time or two, and couldn't make it fit. So we didn't give him any name at all. When we had to speak of him, he was just "the new one" or "the white one."

Then the door was left accidentally ajar, and out he came. He found the food bowls on the counter where the others ate. Both eyes open now, he directed his green stare at the dogs, deciding they were neutral. He went where he pleased. The other cats sang less when they saw him. Sometimes they forgot to sing at all.

Eventually, because life is a game of calculated risks, he rolled on his back in front of the tuxedo cat and put out a paw. Eric, startled, a bit unsure, put out his own. And like small boys wrestling, they tumbled happily across the rug. After that, the singing all but stopped.

"Teddy . . ." my wife said one day. "What do you think of Teddy for a name? He looks a little like a bear." So that was settled.

He liked having a house of his own. He quickly learned to come to lap, to sit on the newspaper as it was being read. He didn't mind not being called by that other name, or that his manner wasn't as kingly or his fur quite as soft as some remembered cat's had been.

It didn't matter that he was just a peasant. Because he knew now that his name was Teddy, and he understood that finally he was home.

23. MEL AND JO

OUR HOUSE GUESTS, Mel and Jo, were the nicest folks imaginable. They'd gotten up at 3 o'clock in the morning and driven all the way from Iowa for a church conference. And exhausted by that long day, they came to spend the night with us.

When you accept the hospitality of strangers, you take pot luck. I can only hope the experience will not cause them to lose interest in religion or become less active in matters Presbyterian.

We were not at home when they arrived. They'd left the meeting sooner than they'd planned, and we were out for dinner with a friend from Africa and a visitor from France. How long they'd been waiting is a bit unclear. Not so long, they said. Their car, with its Iowa license, was parked on the street out front.

My wife leapt out to greet them. I rushed to the

house to get a set of golf clubs the Frenchman was going to take back to his brother in Paris. There was a moment of furious milling on the sidewalk, some people coming in, other people leaving with articles of sport. There was no use trying to explain.

We sat Jo and Mel in the living room, and offered soft drinks. Immediately all the cats appeared — more cats than they'd ever seen in one place. And the enormous one, Teddy, bore immediately for the sofa, where Jo sought to ward him off with discreet little motions of her hand, while at the same time managing to smile and drink her soda.

Mel thought he might take a bath before turning in.

We urged him by all means to feel at home. But it was an old house, we explained, with certain defects. The upstairs bathroom door was hard to close. If you pressed against it — pressed *really hard*, that is — it usually would latch. Otherwise it might swing open.

The tub drain was temperamental, too. Sometimes you had to kind of jiggle it to make it hold water. Sing out if you need help with it, I said. (Although having to ask someone you've known for about 10 minutes to help you take a bath is not one of the easier things to do.)

Oh, yes, we added. The door of the guest bedroom was tricky, too. Wouldn't latch no matter how hard you pushed. It might be a good idea to get inside and put a chair against it, unless they wanted to wake up in the morning with cats sleeping all around and over them.

We said we hoped they didn't have any animal allergies.

"No, no!" they replied brightly, both smiling at once. "We love cats!"

So they retired. And it was time then to bring in the dogs. First came the old one, legs splaying, falling, getting up, wheezing like some emphysemic murderer dragging a body up the stairs. After that it was the bird dog's turn. He always comes in with much commotion, skidding, running into things, nails scraping on the floor, more or less guided by my screams and threats.

It's the sort of terrifying racket you would hear from an inexperienced mahout trying to direct a killer elephant.

Then, for a while, it was silent in the darkness. I imagine our guests caught an uneasy nap. Then a cat knocked a glass off the guest bathroom sink. Then a different cat, lonely on the floor below, set up a sepulchral wailing. Then, somehow, it got to be morning.

Then the bird dog went out with another explosion of noise — past the bathroom, occupied but with its door ajar; past the bedroom, with the chair away from that door and cats boiling in and out like commuters at a train station.

You cannot believe how fast it is possible for people to get dressed, packed and ready for the road. At breakfast, they kept looking alertly around — wondering what might come at them next out of some corner.

We said we hoped they had rested comfortably.

They sure had, Mel said. They'd barred the door, as we advised. Nothing had molested them. And the bed was the healthiest kind to sleep on. Good for the back. Very firm.

It reminded her, Jo said, of a bed they'd slept on once in Mexico.

Then they hurried out to throw suitcase and clothes bag in the back of the car. We liked Mel and Jo a lot. We were glad to have put them up, and just wished they hadn't been so pressed for time.

Our neighbor to the west mentioned afterward that he'd had house guests for a church conference a year or two ago. He was going to be gone a lot, but he told them to help themselves to milk in the refrigerator and cookies in the pantry. Later he discovered they'd gotten the wrong sack, and had spent the weekend eating dog treats.

No one ever promised that the way of faith would be easy.

24. AN ORANGE PERIL

Eric is, I believe, the most intelligent of the cats we've lived with. At least none has been so expressive, or taken so active a role in the affairs of the household.

When not on his window ledge, he is busy regulating disputes among the other cats. If a new stray joins the pride, he is the first to offer a friendly welcome. Besides his gift for diplomacy, he has that rarest of qualities in beasts of any shape, including humans: a sense of humor.

And what proof do I have of all this? You'll simply have to take my word for it, in the same way we accept people's claims about their grandchildren.

Soon after appearing on our doorstep he understood the terms of the deal. In return for a full bowl on the kitchen counter, he would give up the sordid vices of the hunter. He still likes to observe through the window the activity at the bird feeder, but unlike the other cats his teeth no longer grind and click when he watches.

Each morning, before breakfast, he makes a brief patrol of the front porch and the adjoining bushes. Lately I've noticed the yard rabbit venturing nearer and nearer the shrubs where Eric lurks, and I have wondered if instinct might have its way, causing something nasty to happen.

Yesterday morning, I was startled to find the two of them were under the same bush *together*, seeming pleased by their near association. When I called, the rabbit hopped off unalarmed, and Eric came in to his bowl.

Maybe there's nothing to it. One has to be careful about reading too much into so trifling an event. Or it may say something about the civilizing power of a full stomach and a secure place as part of a larger group, and about the ability of creatures gifted in these ways to master their coarser tendencies and live in harmony.

Or it may be that Eric is only exceptional, after all.

But as much as he loves his few minutes abroad in the world, there is one presence he cannot abide. Somewhere out there *the Orange Peril waits!* The provenance of that swaggering beast is unknown. He must be a member of some other household in the neighborhood, for his passage across our lawn is a fairly regular event. At home he may be coddled and adored. Here he is despised.

Eric will be perched on the inner window sill. Then, out of nowhere, the enormous orange tabby will come lumbering by. He looks up at the window. Their stares meet. Eric trembles with fury at the trespass. Once the intruder sprang up to hang by his claws from the window screen. But usually, after determining he's been satisfactorily noticed, the orange one just gives a kind of shrug and passes on.

One morning last week, Eric had gone out with me as he usually does when I fetch the paper. A short time later, as I sat reading over the day's first cup of coffee, there arose from outside the front door a violent commotion — spitting, screeching, yowling, and other noises I hadn't known a cat could make. I flung open the door and Eric came scuttling in, low to the ground.

At the eye's corner, I caught just a glimpse of the orange brute making his hasty way toward other parts. So they'd met whisker to whisker at last. No injuries were detected. The battle seemed to have been mainly one of shouted insults. But it has changed the nature of our mornings.

Each day, since then, Eric has gone to the door as usual, asking for his quarter-hour at large. The door is opened. From the safety of the hall, he peers out with a mix of longing and apprehension. Then, sadly, he turns away.

I understand, and know what he's feeling. Because there was a threat like that in my own early boyhood as well — a boy about my age, but a good deal larger, who found pleasure in deviling me on the way home from school. He'd twist my arm behind my back, and march me all the way to his house before releasing me to flee to mine. Each morning I left for school in an agony of dread, knowing the torment that might wait at the end of the day.

Eventually it stopped. He found another victim, or turned to pulling the legs off bugs. I met that fellow years later, and am glad to say he'd outgrown such meanness. That could happen to the prowling tabby, too, maybe sooner rather than later.

So today, when Eric turned away from the door again in despair, I snatched him up and carried him out onto the stoop. He surveyed the yard. The orange thug was nowhere to be seen. So he went on out, then, and stayed his allotted minutes, and had to be called three times. When finally he came, his manner seemed more confident. There was a bounce in his step. And I suspect he's already looking forward to tomorrow's outing.

For all of us, life contains a variety of terrors — some that are unbearable in the imagining. But they tend to get smaller the sooner you're able to face them.

25. WAIST-WATCHERS

THE NEW WHITE CAT, Teddy, has taken on a fearful lot of weight. It's the result, I think, not so much of gluttony as of a kind of basic confusion about how time passes. He mistakes the minutes for hours, meaning that the interval between meals is greatly shortened. And the effect can be seen in other things as well.

Each morning he joins the crowd of his fellow household creatures, gathered for the jostling rush through the back door out into the dewy wilderness of the yard. His anticipation of that moment obviously is keen.

It isn't a lengthy outing — a few minutes at most. A little grass is eaten. A tree sometimes is climbed. But there's always the chance — the hope, at any rate — that something small and furtive might be spied creeping in the grass.

All the others stay out until they're called. A couple of the more adventurous among them have to be retrieved manually. Not Teddy. Eyes shining, stubby little legs churning, he heaves himself out into the natural world. But in the half-minute it takes to fill the coffeepot and set it heating, he's back again, the novelty of exploring worn off already.

Let inside, he goes directly to his food bowl. Then

he watches the others through the window. And in another couple of minutes it occurs to him that the morning has gotten long, and that it must be lunch time.

It's little errors like that, in men or cats, that cause the waist to disappear.

He came to us from hard times, Teddy did. His great round face was stitched and scarred, and there'd been spells when the meals weren't so regular. His change of luck, when it came, may simply have been too sudden and comprehensive to fully grasp.

One moment he was a wounded refugee, growling to hide his terror, slitted eyes casting around for a threat. The next minute there were cushions and cat-nip on a newspaper on the kitchen floor. And there were benign dogs. And good-humored Eric, who never showed a claw, was inviting him to play.

People took him up and stroked him. A girl crea-ture smoothed his coat with a brush. Strangers arriv-ing at the door saw him and pronounced an unex-pected word: *Beautiful!* And if all that change could occur almost in an eye blink, why wouldn't his whole concept of hours and days be much compressed?

Whenever something nice happens, he celebrates — as any of us would — by hurrying off to get a tasty bite. Which would be fine, if those were occa-sional events. But nice things happen too often. His celebrations are practically continuous.

If you ask me, good luck has permanently disordered the way that Teddy measures time. Woolly coated, broad-backed, solid as a steer, he waddles among us now, covered in great rolls of happiness. *There's not a dark cloud anywhere in sight*, you almost can see him thinking. And immediately he feels an appetite coming on.

2 6 . L O S S E S , G A I N S

THE OLD DOG, CINNAMON, had gotten unsteady on the stairs. For several weeks I carried her up to the bedroom in the evening, and down again in the morning when we woke. We tried to pretend she was only passingly infirm. But in our hearts we knew that she was failing.

She still liked riding to the farm in fine weather. It almost seemed those little outings evoked her recollection of younger years. For immediately when the car door opened she would scamper — or what passed for a matron's scamper — down the wooded lane to the pond.

We worried that the exertion might be too much for her. But then we thought, *what are we saving her for?* She didn't swim there, as she used to love doing, but she waded at the edge.

And that's where we scattered her ashes when she left us.

We miss her. She came to us by chance, as so many do, and was with us through the comings and goings of many cats. One of those, the third Oliver, was her special friend. She endured the arrival of the bird dog, Rufus, who followed her in the yard, puppy jaws clamped on one of her rear legs.

Time goes like smoke, and with our gains and losses the numbers of us in this house are forever changing. Now Rufus is an older dog, and his two sons — orange-and-white Pete and liver-and-white Bear — have taken their places in our tribe.

Pete is the larger and a bit the bolder. Little Bear is soft-natured and playful. Both pups have inherited their father's spirit. And both are respectful and properly admiring of the cats, though I don't know that we'll ever find them napping with a kitty curled in the bend of their bodies, the way Cinnamon and Oliver used to sleep.

But that picture is locked away securely in memory, along with the pictures of all the others who've shared our years. And memory is a dependable steward. The images stored there can be as real as yesterday, as warm as life itself. And they are available any time one has a quiet moment alone.

27. THE PRICE OF CHANGE

TEDDY — A CREATURE OF habit, as are we all — wears a worried look these days. One small change in the arrangement of the kitchen has set his universe on end.

Having no work to do, no mice to catch, and nothing in particular he cares to write, his life centers mainly on the food bowl, a devotion I fully understand and share.

The bowls are aligned atop the counter, to prevent poaching by the pups. At the counter's end, under the shelf that holds the telephone, there used to be a desk with drawers. The other cats levitated easily from floor to the telephone perch, and passed directly from there to nourishment. But Teddy, as his heft increased, required help.

I saw in the news the other day where they had to cut out part of a wall so a man weighing 1,000 pounds could be extracted from his house and gotten to a hospital. No comparison is intended. Teddy is a mere 23-pounder, and "Solid," as my wife likes to say. Still, in describing him, *nimble* is not an adjective that comes to mind.

So a booster chair was placed in front of the desk, enabling him to ascend by stages to the place beside the phone, and thence to his bowl.

But now has come the calamity.

The desk was moved to another room, to make leg space for someone using the telephone, leaving an empty hole. The chair's position is unchanged, and the distance from it to the telephone shelf is the same. But behind the chair, in the place where the desk used to be, there is only that emptiness. The other cats seem not even to have noticed the difference. But this new state of affairs has filled Teddy with ungovernable dread.

You see him sitting in front of the chair, looking up at it, and at the telephone, and beyond that toward the food bowls that are invisible on the countertop. What is he thinking? That he might somehow miss the chair? He has never missed it before, but then there never was that terrible hole behind.

His shoulders and haunches work, as if to leap. He doesn't, though. Like a mountaineer balking before an impossible traverse, he cannot commit. The exposure is too great. In despair, he turns away.

The first few days we lifted him to his food. But that would be unworkable for the long term. Teddy eats often, very often, and it would mean spending most of the rest of our lives in the kitchen.

"He'll find a way to manage," I told my wife.

"I'm not so sure. It frightens him a lot."

"Believe me," I said. "He's making progress. Just

watch this." I opened the door from the back yard, and Pete and Bear, the bird dog brothers, came thundering in.

As if by magic, without even thinking about it or quite understanding how it happened, Teddy found himself atop the counter with the food bowls. And life seemed possible again.

All terrors are relative. Wonderful, isn't it, how a little thing like a couple of rowdy pups can speed the learning curve!

28 . THE PROWLER

A ROCKING CHAIR, A CAT, an empty house. Terror can come in the shape of things you know.

We'd gone out for dessert and coffee. Our daughter was in the kitchen, prospecting in the refrigerator. Home for a visit, she'd come in late and hungry from some errand of her own. Now that we're all more or less autonomous adults, we keep our independent schedules.

She heard the thump of the front door closing.

"Hello," she called out.

We didn't answer.

Then she heard the measured tap of footsteps across the wooden floor.

Without waiting to confront some stranger she

fled through the side door onto the drive. But the season had turned and the night was raw. She circled to the front and looked in through the windows. The stranger could not be seen.

She was cold. Her car keys were on the bench in the hall, in the danger zone. Being alone struck her, in that moment, as most unattractive. She was thinking with sudden fondness of the companionship of the college dorm to which she would soon return.

But she is not uncourageous. So she crept around to the side and back into the kitchen without making a sound. She took a granola bar from the cupboard for provisions, and her coat from the back of the chair, and had nearly convinced herself the place was safe — when she saw *THE SHAPE*.

It was visible just on the other side of the louvered door between the kitchen and breakfast room. So she fled into the hall and snatched up her car keys. Then bolted out to the car, locked herself inside and huddled there, grimly gnawing the granola bar, waiting to see who or what would come out of the house.

No one did. We came home and found her there, a small, sad exile, alone in the night in the car on the drive.

I went inside first, alone — an ostentatious show of bravery, but a hollow one, since I knew all about this intruder. I'd heard him many times before.

There's a rocking chair in which the big cat Teddy likes to sleep. Bounding down whenever something wakes him and he remembers food, he sets the chair in motion. If it happens to be drawn too near the corner of the room, its back strikes the wall.

I gave the chair a little push. "What do you hear?"

"That's the door closing."

It's a heavy old chair, the one my grandfather used to keep beside his fireplace. Once moving, it takes a while to stop. The rockers thumped out a sinister rhythm.

"Those are the footsteps," she said.

And *THE SHAPE?*

A cat, she decided. Just the round shadow of it, like the feet of someone standing at the door — Teddy or one of the others, peering through the crack at the food bowls on the kitchen counter, concerned that the way to nourishment was blocked.

When you've been away at school, with a dormitory room all to yourself, it takes a while to relearn the sounds and habits of a place crowded with so many lives. Around her here, a lot of things go bump in the night. So far, the prowler has always been one of us.

29. A TROPHY CAT

NOW TEDDY IS ON A DIET,.and it's a trial for everyone in the house. He did not choose this thorny path of self-improvement. Who ever does? He was forced to walk it.

"Do you know how much Teddy weighs?" our daughter asked.

"Twenty-three pounds," I replied. "The size of a supermarket frozen turkey, more or less."

"More."

"Well, that was his last weigh-in — 23, right on the mark."

"It's 26 now."

"Good. Only four more to go. I would like to be able to say I once owned a 30-pound cat — a *trophy* cat."

"He's put on three more pounds in a year."

"That's not so much," I said.

"Are you kidding? At that rate, in five years he'll weigh more than the bird dog."

"Teddy is big-boned," my wife put in. "He carries it well."

The truth is, he rarely carries it at all. Mostly he puts it in a chair and leaves it there. His legs have all but disappeared.

"The diet starts tomorrow," our daughter declared

flatly. "There's special food for cats with a severe eating disorder like his."

"It can't be done," we protested. "What about all the other cats?"

"We'll figure out a way," she said.

And we have, sort of. But it is incredibly complicated. They are used to eating, all of them, at bowls arranged on the kitchen counter. Now we have to segregate them. The trouble is that several of them have learned to open the kitchen door.

So when the others are eating, Teddy's food bowl is on the floor in the outer hall and the door is secured with heavy rubber bands. Lest he sink into deep depression, it is necessary from time to time to carry his bowl back to the counter so he may take nourishment in the familiar place, and to put theirs on the floor outside.

Teddy is disgusted by his slimming ration, although it is the same in shape and texture as the regular food, differing only slightly in color.

The others, noticing the special treatment he is receiving, naturally have decided that his food is uncommonly desirable, and they miss no opportunity to poach at his bowl.

No matter which food is on the floor in the hall, it lies in the immediate trajectory of the bird dog, Rufus, on his careens between the back yard and the chair in the upstairs bedroom. And Rufus considers both brands superior to his own, although three of the cats would prefer to eat dog food if they were allowed.

The management of all this is like one of those thought problems that used to defeat me in grade school arithmetic. One of us, my wife or I, must spend a good deal of time closed up in the kitchen, shouting out into the house for the other to come take the rubber bands off the door.

But it seems to be paying off. He is down three pounds, to 23 again, and last night we noticed that Teddy's legs had reappeared. We have begun to detect flatter places at the sides, although the impression he gives still is largely spherical.

And best of all, he is markedly more active. We're apt to see him now almost anywhere in the house. Yesterday he was upstairs several times.

I wouldn't exactly say he frolics. His brow is furrowed. He moves with purpose. He knows we're operating at the very edge of our administrative competence, and that sometime, somewhere, we'll make a mistake with the bowls.

30 . THREE KITTENS

WHAT'S A SUFFICIENCY of cats? We don't know yet, but surely we are feeling our way toward it, if we're not there already. The latest are three kittens, arrived from the farm just as the first hard spell of weather came on. We must try to find them homes.

We have had kittens before, but never so many at once. This is different. The pleasure of the gang of them together is greater than three times one. So far we've not had the nerve to unleash them into the larger tribe. Their universe has been bounded by the walls of our bedroom and bath. Washing oneself in the tub while three little cats are trying to get in the water with you is an adventure to be undertaken sparingly.

What that means, in the days between, is that you must move slowly, try never to perspire, and accept few social engagements.

Mornings are best. While I am letting the dogs out and boiling coffee water, my wife opens the bathroom door and the rascals charge forth rested and ready to begin a romp. From the breakfast room on the floor below, I can hear them up there — feet drumming like the hooves of little horses. Then I carry my coffee up, and settle in a chair to watch the chases and pounces.

Their games are a good deal fairer and better-natured than the ones I remember from my days on the grade school playground. They make a great show of ferocity. But when wrestling, each is careful to let the others have a turn at winning.

The sound of a radio they do not notice. One played continually in the shed where they were born and spent their first days. Nor are they alarmed by dogs, since two gentle, woolly ones were part of their early experience.

We used to watch morning television sometimes. But the combination of voices and flashing picture terrifies them and sends them under the bed. So we've given it up.

The play time lasts the better part of the morning. Then one becomes aware finally of an unnatural silence overhead. Creep up to the bedroom and you find them sleeping, recovering from all that exercise. Sometimes they are curled in chairs and on dresser tops and in a dog basket. Often they are all together in one knot on the bed itself.

That's how the afternoon mostly passes. By evening they're recharged, ready for another round of play before being closed away for the night. And somewhere in all this, they find time to eat a stupendous amount of food, causing themselves to grow at an amazing rate. When they came, any one of them would fit in the palm of your hand. In just weeks, they're already adolescents.

The idea at the beginning was only to get them their shots, fatten them up a bit, then give them away. Lately, though, the last part of the plan is less talked about. Who would take all three? And how could such small friends be separated?

In that morning hour, when I get up from watching them, no matter what the day holds I feel light and young. What would replace that? Probably we'd go back to listening to the morning talk-show jabber, and I'd have to start bathing regularly again.

"How many would we have if we could?" I asked my wife the other night.

"How many what? Cats?"

We were talking in the dark, softly, so as not to disturb the sleeping nursery.

"I don't know," she said, and thought about it. "Maybe we should live in the country and have a barn. Then there'd be no upper limit."

It would be a big step. I'm attached to the house we live in, and we like the neighbors. Probably it will never happen. But it's a fine thing to imagine at the very edge of sleep — the way some people think about what it would be like to win the lottery.

3 1 . BLAME GENETICS

I HAVE A THEORY, WHICH I believe competent research will one day bear out, that some people exude an aura — an attraction of some sort — to which homeless cats are drawn like iron filings to a magnet, or moths to a light.

It is a trait that, like certain other disabilities, seems to be transmitted primarily on the maternal side of the lineage. Persons afflicted by it do not seek out cats. They only need to pass along a street or a country lane, especially as winter starts to turn. And immediately cats appear out of barns, bushes, trash bins and from under abandoned cars to declare their availability and great need.

I discovered, too late, that the woman I married possessed this disorder. Our daughters, especially the younger one, seem to have inherited it in alarming degree. Carriers of the gene can be lovely and agreeable people in every other way, but living with them keeps you always on edge. As with reformed gamblers or kleptomaniacs, you never know when life might take another ugly turn.

Our daughter, the one who has the *cattraction* ailment the worst, was at large in the city the other evening. She telephoned home just at the supper hour. Her mother answered, so I heard only one side of the conversation.

"Where was he?"

"Where was who?" I asked. But I was out of the loop, as they say. The sick were talking between themselves.

"That's a dangerous street," said my wife. "It's a miracle he wasn't hit."

"Who wasn't hit?" I asked, and was ignored.

"Did you ask around the neighborhood?"

A pause.

"And they moved out and left him? That's rotten."

A longer pause.

"Came right to you, did he? Wrapped himself around your legs?"

No!" I cried.

It was as if I had not spoken.

"Yes, of course, bring him," my wife was saying. "We'll find a place."

"Please, heaven. Not another one!"

She hung up the phone.

"What in the world are you doing?" she asked.

"I can't take it," I said. "I'm putting my head in the oven and turning on the gas."

"The oven's electric."

"Then it's no use, is it?"

"None at all," she said. "The cat carrier's in the

basement. We'll need it to bring him from the car."

So the cat came home to join us, as all of them eventually do. He was a fine beast, about half-grown, sleek and shiny as a seal. He'd done all right for himself, living on the street.

"It's only temporary," my wife said. She remembered how, earlier that same day, friends had mentioned losing their cat to an illness. "Maybe they'll take him."

"I don't know," I told her.

"What do you mean, *you don't know?*" she said.

"I'm not sure what I mean, exactly. All I'm saying is he looks like a pretty outstanding cat."

"You want to keep him."

"No," I lied. "Keeping him is out of the question."

"But you're thinking it."

It was true, and that's the worst part. Within families, even those who don't carry the gene for attracting cats can be seen to display some of the later symptoms of the disease. And it can go on like that for generations — an endless cycle, for which research may show the only remedy to be neutering.

3 2 . L O V E   O F   F I R E

THERE'S NOTHING THE LITTLE gray cat, Roosevelt, likes quite as much as a fire.

We enjoy fires, too, and have had quite a few of them on chilly nights of this deepening autumn. But for Roosevelt it's more than just enjoyment. Her fascination with fire is almost sensual — the nearest thing to excitement she displays.

She's gotten on to middle age now, a solemn creature and very dear. But not, if truth be told, awfully bright. She was orphaned as a kitten, near an orchard where she spent her first weeks in the company of rabbits and hounds.

Early hunger stunted her growth, and may have made her a bit slow as well. Sometimes she gets lost in the house where she's lived all her years, and emits cries of lonely desperation, not remembering how to get to the next room where the people are.

But put her before the fireplace screen when a blaze is flickering on the hearth and her focus is absolute.

She will sit there for hours, motionless as the ceramic cat we once had on the table of our rented apartment in Paris. Her gray coat shines silver in the reflected light. She absorbs the radiant heat until she is almost too hot to touch. And still she sits, unmoving.

If it becomes necessary to put on another log, you have to lift her, set her aside, then put her back afterward. She seems to be in a trance — rigid as those ladies that stage magicians levitate with a wand.

Her yellow eyes are fixed, unblinking, on the color and brightness and the rise and fall of the tongues of flame. It's clear in those times that what she has of intellect is totally engaged.

Is she remembering her own cold beginning? Or thinking of all the others not lucky enough to have found their way into someone's apple basket and through a friendly door?

Or is some older, wilder part of her looking farther back than that, and seeing in the movement of fire-light the shadows of her ancient kin — the ones who first came out of the secret darkness and took the risk of being kept?

Whatever she spies there, it holds her powerfully. Until the last red coals have faded and the fire has fallen away to white ash she remains there at her station.

Then she rises with regret. The confusion returns. And like a traveler suddenly without a compass, she wanders away into the house, whose map she cannot seem to learn. The other cats may be more capable, but they have no passion that burns as fiercely as hers.

33. TRAVEL TALES

IN THIS CHANGEABLE SEASON, one morning is frigid, the next mild. And Eric waffles between his devotion to the radiator top and the lust for his morning excursion in the yard.

It is not so much *being* out that seems to matter. It's the fact of having *been* out that gives him status. The other cats are waiting when he swaggers through the door. They sniff him head and tail and are impressed.

The limit of their world is the fenced back yard. But because of Eric's dependability and his willingness to come when called, his travels are more exotic — to the bushes outside the front door. The smell of the great unknown is on him.

He is the one who goes places, while they, the homebodies, have to live vicariously.

It's like being at a party where someone has just gotten back from Europe. The traveler doesn't have to announce it. He has a certain look about him, a certain carriage. People *know*.

"Yesterday," someone whispers. "He just came back yesterday."

In fact, the traveler may have had a rotten time. He may have gotten dysentery in Portugal, been overcharged in Paris and had his suitcase stolen in Rome, but these are incidents of which it is not necessary to speak.

"Fabulous," he says. "The weather was fine." Though the truth is it rained every day but one.

There's admiration and a little envy in the air.

That's how it is when Eric comes back indoors. All he has really done is crouch under his bush, trembling with cold and thinking of his bowl the way travelers to other, grander places think of cheeseburgers and their beds at home.

The others can't know that, though. All they know is that his fur is rich with the perfume of the fabulous *Out There*. So they gather round deferentially. His standing among them is very large.

Now this is fine in the sweet springtime and the golden days of autumn, and bearable even in the deep of summer. The problem is that winter comes and, no matter how nasty or dark the morning, he has to do it. Because in order to *have been out* it's necessary first actually to *go* out. He's trapped by this pose he's struck and by the sense the others have of him.

Probably you've known people like that. Folks do things they'd rather not do, or behave in ways they know are foolish or risky, just because it's what they've done for so long that people expect it of them.

"He's always been a fighter," someone will say. So, naturally, he has to pick a fight.

One night recently the temperature sank away into the middle teens, and in the morning Eric was scratching at the door.

"You're not going to like it out there," I told him. I think he knew that already — could feel the cold seeping in over the threshold. But there was no choice. He had to do it.

About two minutes later, without being called, he was scratching to be let back in. The others gathered round, admiring as ever. And though his feet were cold, his celebrity was intact.

As any experienced adventurer can tell you, it's where you've come back from that gets you noticed, not what happened there or how long you stayed.

34. A TRUCE

AFTER FIVE YEARS OF loathing and intimidation, the white cat, Teddy, and the pied one, Felix, suddenly have declared a truce.

It happened in the season of kindness, at the time of making new resolutions. And there's no account for it. It's a miracle, that's all — like the leopard changing spots, or the lion lying down with the lamb, or Ariel Sharon hugging Yasser Arafat.

"They're touching noses," cried a voice from the

kitchen.

"Who is?"

"Felix and Teddy. I just saw them do it."

"Don't make sick jokes."

"No, it's true. Come see for yourself."

Felix, the spotted one, is 15 or possibly 16 years old and arboreal. He lives on top of the stove, takes his meals on the counter top and has not voluntarily descended to the floor since the white cat, Teddy, joined the family.

Comparatively speaking, Teddy is a youngster, though handicapped by his great girth. But inside the bulk of him is a faint heart. Despite having once out-stared the neighbor's dog, Felix really is timid, too, and that may be the root of the problem. Each sees in the other a mirror image of his own nature and is moved by that to anger and contempt.

Their habit has been to lurk.

Teddy would enter the kitchen and, while pondering how he might levitate his considerable self to the counter and the food bowl, would notice Felix peering down malignly from above. His appetite would leave him, and he would withdraw with a little groan of despair.

Felix, wondering what it might be like to pass some time as other cats do, on the ground instead of up with the pans and teapot, would advance to the stove's edge.

And just as he was screwing up his nerve to bound down, he would see the face of the enemy — or *half* of it, like a great white risen moon — glowering one-eyed, one-eared around the corner of the door.

In the first years they sometimes got careless in the night. Evidently there were accidental meetings, because at first light we would find scatterings of hair tufts — the kind of grim residue you see on the veldt, where the swift afoot have caught up with some straggler of the herd.

Now, quite suddenly, the drama of their lives is subtracted. Teddy enters the kitchen when it pleases him. Felix has been noticed to walk directly past him, leap down from counter to chair and chair to floor and stroll away with the air of lofty dignity that is the entitlement of his years.

That first unexplainable gesture has ripened into what seems a benign indifference. They are careful not to let their eyes directly meet. Both of them seem to sleep a lot, as if exhausted by their years of fury and glad to have it done with.

Chums they aren't, not yet at least. But out of such small triumphs of civility — in our kitchen, or in some of the more hateful places of the world — anything might grow.

35. GIFTS ENOUGH

I STILL REMEMBER HOW the excitement used to build. Each box was shaken, smelled, its heft assayed, to see if inside the bright wrapping there might be a particular wish answered, some item from the list of wanted things.

The night was endless, time's slow passage marked by a hundred fitful wakings. Then the window lightened. Then there was the rattle of the old coal furnace being shaken. Then soft voices from the kitchen. Then a footstep, a hand on the knob of the door.

And after that agony of waiting, whose intensity and duration only a child can ever really know, the morning — important above all others — began at last.

You get older, though. We all do. The impatience and the expectation subside and are replaced, with luck, by a sense not of yearning but of *completion*. And by the understanding that satisfaction of the longer kind comes in shapes that cannot be boxed and wrapped.

Not many years ago we spent this season in a little mountain village in Italy — a place that, when we arrived there in the frosty night, smelled of straw and horses and chocolate.

The snow was deep, the cold fierce. On that Christmas Eve we walked with our daughters and some friends down the lane from the hotel at the upper edge of the town, past the little church with a blue neon angel on the steeple. The people in the church were singing, and as we stood listening our breath made frosty plumes in the frozen dark.

Then we went on down together to the steep street of the town where the shops still were open, though it was nearly midnight, and a lighted cafe was serving cappuccino and spiced hot cider and stronger things to drive out the chill.

It's possible there were some presents exchanged that Christmas morning — small things brought with us, tucked in a suitcase's corner. But if there were, I honestly don't remember. What I do remember is the sense of waking in that place together, in chilly rooms a long way from home, and knowing as my first thought of Christmas morning that I had, then, everything I wanted or would ever need.

It's the same feeling I had last night, after an evening spent in companionship and easy talk with some of our oldest friends.

The house had emptied. The fire had burned down. Under the tree were the packages, waiting to be opened on this day. But my interest in their contents, I have to say, was of a mild and easy kind, unlikely to interfere at all with sleeping.

Because, again, there was nothing left to need.

Across the miles and through the almost unimaginable hazards of these times, our daughters had been delivered safely home to us. To be sure of that, I stood a few moments in the darkness of their rooms, just to listen to the soft breathing of them in their dreams.

Shortly I would lie down next to the woman with whom I have spent more than half the years of my life — a friend who knows me better than I know myself, and cares in spite of that.

The dogs were sleeping in their chairs.

The many cats were warm on the tops of radiators.

The door was latched. The ancient furnace thrummed against the outer cold. Photographs of our remembered moments looked down from the walls. We were as safe in that place, in that moment, as living things can ever be.

And we were together.

Never mind, I thought, what might be in those packages still to be unwrapped. At a certain time of life, you go to your bed in the stillness of Christmas Eve, and if you are incredibly, undeservedly lucky you already have the gifts you wanted — or else you know it's too late to ask.

36 . OUT OF SCHOOL

TWO KITTENS CAME HOME from college for the holiday — Spanky, a calico, and a shiny black one with golden eyes, named Headlight. And now the question, still unspoken, hangs darkly over us. Will the cats go back to resume their educations? Or has the population of our our household taken a further, permanent leap?

The holiday is a long one, so it's a fortnight yet before the issue has to be faced head-on. Meantime, the established resident cats try to pretend this hasn't happened. They do not crouch singing at the closed bedroom door. Nor have they turned on one another. Or gone into a frenzy of disemboweling cushioned chairs and marking territory. The only sign of despair is a slight irritability.

The dogs are genuinely indifferent. As far as they are concerned, one cat is about like the next 10 or 12. Smell one, you've smelled them all.

The new lodgers were allowed downstairs on Christmas morning. They examined the tree, helped open a package or two, did a little timid exploring. The old cats sat with their eyes fixed levelly on some point in the far distance. Then the new ones were taken back upstairs, and life resumed.

Most of the time I am able to forget that they are

with us. Somewhere I have read that cats sleep 18 hours a day. The other six hours, since these are college cats, they probably spend in quiet reading, keeping their minds sharp for the start of the new semester.

Only in the morning do they make their presence known. First there are two soft thumps on the floor above — their quarters being directly over the breakfast room.

"They're up," my wife announces.

Then comes a prolonged scuffling sound, as if a herd of very small reindeer in bedroom slippers had begun galloping around up there. Then there is a bang as something falls. More scuffling. Then multiple bangs.

"Right," I say. "They're up."

None of this racket seems to interfere with the sleep of their mistresses, the vacationing students. Lumpish under blankets, they are far gone in dreams. For all I know, they could be dreaming of more cats. But who can say? The noise cannot touch them. Tomorrow will take care of itself.

How I wish I could believe that!

"Where does it end?" I ask.

My wife, her coffee cup suspended, looks up from the morning paper.

"What end?"

"Cats," I say. "What's to become of us?"

"Maybe we'll find homes for them."

"Hah!" I reply huskily. That's what is said every time a new one comes. *Maybe we'll find it a home.* But it's a meaningless phrase. Home already has been found.

"The girls have more years of college ahead," I say. "And after that, maybe graduate school. If they keep bringing home cats, think of the fix we'll be in."

"Don't borrow trouble before it comes," she says. "Anyway, these two were small. And very deserving."

There is another, larger crash from the room above.

"Ah, yes," I murmur, and wander off to look for a sofa without some animal on it, where I can curl in a fetal position.

As I've said before, the sickness is inherited. My wife carries the deadly gene. It all began a long time before cats or daughters were born, and there is not, in our lifetimes, the faintest hope of a cure.

37. TWO GO, TWO STAY

WITH BREATHTAKING suddenness, the house has emptied out.

Well, not emptied, exactly. Two cats brought home for a Christmas visit decided, at the last minute, to suspend their careers as scholars. So they remain, finding their places in the hierarchy of our jungle, exploring a kingdom wider than a dormitory room.

Only our daughters have gone back to school, and the sensation is — what? A bit of lonesomeness. Also, to be honest, some guilty relief.

The hours they keep in that other place, the clothes they wear, their wakings-up, the friends they cultivate — it's all beyond any control of ours, and thus no part of our responsibility. We do not listen for a car on the drive, the turn of the door latch. The only itinerary that rules us is our own.

That is the happy part. The other part is the vacancy of the rooms they briefly occupied again, and the sense of things planned that went undone in the rush of the crowded season.

Hardly any memories are left. A few snatched meals together. A day's walking across winter-barren fields. A drive to the airport. The blurred image of them vanishing down the boarding ramp on the other side of the glass. They even carried away with them the few photographs we made. And though I meant to do it, probably I'll never get the duplicates printed.

On the other hand, having seen them to their plane, their mother and I went off to lunch together with a kind of giddy lightness. And talked for hours in the most irresponsible and uninterrupted way. And decided, just on impulse, to see an afternoon movie. And afterward sat over coffee in a cafe to talk some more.

Some scenes of the movie had been set in Paris, on

a street we thought we recognized, and those sparked some old yearnings. Maybe we should just throw everything over and go live there again, I declared. It might even be, she said, that our same apartment from the last time would be available.

When you're on your own, without responsibilities, crazy notions like that come over you.

It's all illusion, of course. Behind the venerable walls of that distant school there sits a bursar, his eyes flinty as a croupier's, waiting to collect the earnings of the rest of my natural life. I tried joking with him once — volunteered to donate, by contract, one of every organ of which I have two. He didn't smile.

So I'm stuck with regular work, but at least, with the girls gone, I once more have a car to take me to it, instead of standing in the weather pathetically at the curb, on the chance someone I know might pass that way and drive me home.

That night, after a whole day's travel, their voices came thin across the wire from half a continent away.

"We're here," they said.

"Good," we replied. "And we're here."

"I'll bet you're awfully lonely," they said.

"It's not so bad. We lost two, but we gained two — two cats. That's a reasonable trade."

They knew we didn't mean it, I'm sure. But you could have counted to 50 in the silence on the wire.

38. YOUTH REMEMBERED

IN THE DARK OF THE year, the house is alight with a kind of energy that the electric company doesn't charge for. The two kittens are teaching the old cats to be young again.

For the first few months their world was a dorm room. Now it's the larger jungle of halls and stairs, over which, almost without challenge, they've claimed dominion.

The midnight black one, Headlight, stalks butterflies on the wallpaper, chases shadows. The other, Spanky, a cat of many colors, pursues her tail a while — then, quick as a sunbeam, flashes through a room and levitates to the top of a cupboard, finds a basket, and perches inside it, just her ears and wide eyes showing, like a nestling waiting for a worm.

The old cats hummed songs of resentment. Then, understanding they were not being replaced, only *added to*, they watched with solemn bafflement these detonations of merriment. And, timidly at first, they began to join the kitten games.

Toys that lay forgotten for years have been rediscovered. Nights, which used to be for sleeping, are the prowling time again. At the edge of dreams, we hear bumps from the room below, and start up alarmed, wondering if some enemy's men are at the door. Then we hear the rocking chair set up its rhythmic thumping. Then the piano booms out a jangling chord.

No pencil can remain unmolested on a desk or table. No book or newspaper can be read without interference. No chair can be sat in without the sitter looking first to see how many are there before him. Everything, for a kitten, is material either for comfort or adventure.

And in the afternoons, when the winter light falls warm through a window onto the carpet, you see them tumbling there in a knot, old cats and small ones together, playing a wrestling game with eyes that glitter and claws kept sheathed.

The kittens are not yet quite tame. Hold them, and you can feel the electricity running — the impatience to quit wasting time on sentiment and get on with all the mischief still undone. The young of most species burn that hotly. And odd as it seems now, I suppose I once did, too.

But time is the great civilizer. Let a few years pass — 40 or 50, say — and the playfulness gets wrung out of you. Duty regulates your hours. Sleep, that once was sweet, only lessens fatigue so that duty may be resumed again. Joy is a full food bowl at the end of another day when you were not run over by a truck.

No doubt the two kittens will come to that in time. But while the fire still is in them, it is amazing to see their effect on the temperaments of the rest of us.

Birds at the back-door feeder, watched through the glass, excite the young hunters' hearts the way that I remember a wedge of geese, passing high across a far sandbar at a frozen river's bend, once excited mine — the better for being unattainable.

The roughhouse on the rug reminds the old cats, as I am reminded, of how fine it used to be to test ourselves, without real wounds ever being dealt, preparing for those later times when the contests would be mortal and the hurts slow to heal.

The explorations in the dark house at small hours suggest there were — and may still be — better uses for the nights than sleeping them away.

All these memories and suspicions the kittens have evoked. By seeing life as entirely new, they *make* it new. After these, I expect, there will be other ones. And others after those. Endlessly. Until one day, possibly, there will be grandchildren. And with that gift, I'm told by experts in the matter, youth comes back to stay.

3 9 . BEAUTIFUL AGAIN

IN THAT OTHER LIFE CALLED youth, he was the Trophy Cat — already of great girth, broad-jowled and intimidating, but with the heart of a lamb.

He came to us, shaved and stitched, from his failure as a barn cat among more capable warriors. The other creatures of our house took one look, recoiled, and sang their song of terror.

Then we discovered there was no meanness in him, and he was assigned the name Teddy to suit his gentle nature.

That was a dozen autumns ago, he was 3 then, and having finally found his right place in the world, he prospered. More accurately, he *inflated* — topped out at 26 pounds, and walked with that delicate, rolling gait of people who once displayed themselves at carnivals but now appear on daytime talk shows instead.

In a house of several cats, try putting one of them on a diet sometime.

You will find yourself with an interesting logistical problem. We tried switching them all to a low-calorie ration. They sulked and declared a fast.

I remember once, when Teddy was in his prime, how a first-time visitor spied him lounging on a chair and cried, in a tone of pure wonder, "What a *beautiful* white cat!" There's no knowing what the visitor really meant to say. But in that instant of astonishment, "beautiful" was the word that came out. With time's passage, the weight was gradually less. What had been 26 pounds became 16. Would that age had such a beneficent effect on us all.

Then, more than a year ago, maybe nearer two, change of a different kind set in. Patches of white fur were found about the house. Pink skin began showing through. A physical found him to be generally sound. He had no fleas, and tests revealed no allergies. Yet plainly he was in discomfort that could be relieved only partly by oatmeal baths.

He lost condition alarmingly. Every bone could be felt. The once-robust white lion had become a fragile, half-naked thing, more pink than white. We resigned ourselves to the prospect of losing him, as eventually one must with these creatures whose lives are shorter than our own.

One morning, though, I saw him at the food bowl and he appeared to have trouble chewing. So we changed him to a soft ration, fed in a closed room apart from the others. He was appreciative at first, but then rejected that, too.

Yet another examination — the fourth or fifth — finally uncovered the problem. Four abscessed teeth had caused him much pain and had sent poison through his system. We felt a wrench of guilt. But when, honestly, does one think to inspect a cat's mouth?

The offending teeth were extracted, the jaw treated, and Teddy came home with an antibiotic. Immediately the healing set in. He'll never be a 26-pound trophy cat again. But his appetite's returned, and each day he's a bit less a bag of bones. The other morning I saw him playing with his best friend, Eric, the two of them standing on their haunches, sparring good-naturedly.

That same day, as we were talking with a visitor in the front hall, Teddy appeared around the corner from another room. His coat has begun growing back, so the worst of his shameful nakedness is covered. But he still has a moth-eaten look that is, to put it generously, somewhat arresting.

"My!" exclaimed our visitor. "What a beautiful white cat!"

I could have wept to hear it. There's no knowing what she really intended to say, but that was the word that came out.

40. HEADLIGHT

THE EYES OF THE BLACK cat, Headlight, are enormous in his face as he follows the flicker of sun and leaf-shadow through the kitchen window, playing against floor and wall.

He is fascinated by the season's changing light. And it reminds us that, alike as creatures may seem, they experience the world in different ways, as individuals.

Many cats, for example, and most dogs, cannot register their reflections in a mirror. But some will sit for an hour before the glass, inclining their heads, reaching out to bat at what they see there, trying to persuade the stranger to come forth.

Some see nothing recognizable in the diminished images on the television screen. To them, it is only sound and meaningless confusion. Others, a few, watch TV the way people do and, like some people, appear to mistake it for life.

From earliest kittenhood, the black cat always has been a little strange. It terrifies him to be touched. Reach out to stroke him and he shrinks away like some victim of habitual abuse, though he's never felt a blow. Attempt to pick him up and the odds are you'll need reconstructive surgery, for the knives he keeps hidden in those black paws are longer and sharper than a Turkish infantryman's.

His is a largely private and internal life.

He will imagine some movement in a figure of the wallpaper, and wait with infinite patience for it to move again. If someone passes through a room, lamplight throwing a shadow ahead, he's apt to ignore the person and pursue the shadow.

Yesterday I was sitting in a chair beside the phone table, talking with my wife and twirling my eyeglasses in my hands. A ray of sunlight refracted by one of the lenses threw a dot of concentrated brilliance on the cabinet beside me. He crouched, eyes tracking that nimble speck with fierce intensity. I stopped twirling the glasses and prayed he would not notice them. It would be hard to type with both hands bandaged.

If I make him out to be unlikable, I don't mean to. He is only strange, and also I believe *lonely* because of not knowing how to receive affection — a tragic disability that some people have as well.

Apart from shadow games, his chief pleasure is to lie perfectly still in an unlighted hallway or at the bottom of the stair, in some place where his blackness is invisible against the dark wood floors. Sooner or later, someone will come that way, stumble over him and nearly fall, and give a little cry of surprise and apology. And he will rush away importantly, then, his existence confirmed by causing himself to be trod upon.

I don't know what shaped his nature, but he is making a connection in the only way he knows. Some of us are just better than others at hiding our timid hearts.

41 . ABANDONED !

A TELEPHONE CALL brought news of the emergency. A cat had been abandoned — a young, unneutered female in heat, terrified, left behind by the woman who'd quit the apartment.

It would give me enormous satisfaction to track that wretched woman to wherever she has gone and identify her to the proper authorities — if there were such — as someone not ever again to be trusted in any matter large or small. Certainly not to be trusted with the care of anything alive.

Behavior like that reveals a great deal about character. And like bad credit or conviction for a crime, the record of it ought to follow one through life.

So now the cat crept in and out through a door left ajar, crying at other tenants' windows, no doubt pursued by the roaming, uncared-for toms belonging in a casual way to other careless lodgers of that neighborhood, or to no one.

That's how it goes for animals that are invited in to share a life, then, when the sharing is inconvenient, are summarily cast out again. It appears that responsibility for dealing with this case of abandonment has fallen, by default, to us. We'll capture the frightened creature, pay to have the necessary surgery performed. And in time we'll find it a home, as we have for so many others before.

Intending to perform an act of mercy is one thing, however. Actually *doing* it can be a different and more complicated matter.

In the first days, the little female — smooth-haired and black — came and went at will from the deserted apartment through a door onto an upstairs stoop. Food and water put out for her were eaten and drunk. But rarely could the actual cat be seen, and then only outside the window atop an air conditioner that tilted dangerously toward an alleyway three floors below.

On a day when she was not visible on that tenuous perch, and thus had to be somewhere in the apartment, the door to the outside was closed and the openings at the sides of the air conditioner were blocked to prevent egress. Now only one large room and the kitchen were available to her. But though the place was empty except for a broken couch and a litter of trash on the floor, no cat could be found.

So we were back there yet again, with a flashlight, and a mirror taped to a pole, and were able to look behind the refrigerator, the stove and the heating unit in a cramped closet. No cat. My eye fell on the derelict couch.

"You don't suppose . . ." I said. We turned the thing upside down. Nothing.

"She must have gotten in the ductwork," declared my wife. We looked at the heat outlets, high on the walls of every room.

"Then we can't get her," I said.

"Maybe the maintenance people can."

"Maybe." Though I couldn't see how, and was becoming depressed, as I suppose preachers sometimes do, by this indifference to the offer of salvation.

I slumped onto the couch. Whereupon the cat squirted out from the couch's deepest innards —

from someplace we couldn't see when we'd turned the thing over. For more than a week, that had been her secret nest. She stared at us owl-eyed for a couple of seconds, then fled through the bathroom door, left open in the latest search, and took refuge under the claw-footed bathtub.

We'd come this time with padded coats and heavy gloves, equipped for serious battle. Unseen and unfindable, the creature had become enormous in our minds. But though she roared at us in terror from under the tub, when finally touched she neither scratched nor bit — just gave in, at last.

A short car ride later and she was installed with us here at home, in a room apart from the others of our cat tribe, with her own food dish, water bowl, litter box, and a soft towel to sleep on. Another 15 minutes after that, having decided her ordeal was over, she was purring softly, happy to be held, lifting her face to touch noses.

As I write this, she's in the care of our veterinarian, Dan, who guesses her to be about a year old, though she weighs but 5 pounds and is hardly bigger than a kitten. With proper food, he says, she'll fill out into a larger cat.

She's been tested and pronounced free of diseases, been wormed and started on her shots. Tomorrow she'll have the surgery to protect her permanently from pursuit by amorous toms. A few days more and she'll be a valued member of some household where the importance of small lives is understood.

And getting left behind by that wretched woman will turn out to have been her greatest luck.

42. HIS NIGHT OUT

HEADLIGHT HAS NEVER cared much for the out-of-doors. When the others make their morning sortie into the back yard, Headlight hesitates on the threshold. If he does decide to go, always he's the first one back.

He recalls his life's first spell of homelessness. And he takes no chances.

Which made his recent disappearance more alarming. The others, after their brief excursion, returned or were gathered in. But Headlight was not among them. Maybe we had misremembered. Could it be he had stayed in that day? Closets were opened, beds looked under, even the nightmare basement searched. No doubt about it, the herd remained one short.

Then a rain came up. Just a spatter of drops at first, then a torrent that fell intermittently through the day and on into evening. Between the downpours, we cruised the neighborhood on foot and by car, peering under bushes, hoping to see a darker shadow move, or the startled shine of golden eyes. But he had vanished utterly. At least, we told ourselves, he hadn't been flattened in the street.

"He's holed up in a dry place somewhere," my wife said. "He'll come back when he's ready. Cats do that."

She is the resident authority, and she said it bravely. But her voice had an edge of worry she couldn't hide. And every quarter-hour or so, she could be heard at the door or out on the lawn, calling the name of the lost.

"Even with people," she said, "the police don't consider them missing until they've been gone overnight."

"Yes," our daughters replied. "But he's never even left the yard before." And they set forth again, this time with friends, to look in all the likely places already looked in.

Where do cats go when, as sometimes happens, the immensity of the universe just swallows them up without a trace, without a hiccup? One minute they are there. An instant later they are gone, fled into some other dimension of space and time — with a finality that makes you start to wonder, crazily, if there ever *really was* such a cat, or if it was only a creature imagined.

That happened once before to us. We liked to tell ourselves — and tell each other — the cat had just decided for some reason unknown, to change houses. "They sometimes do that, too," my wife said. That has been five years ago, and we prefer to believe it still.

The explanation comforts, but it does not compensate. And there is, I suspect, some small erosion of credibility each time it has to be used.

Life goes on, though. The resident authority and I went out to a movie. Our daughters stayed home with friends. Coming back late, we found the friends gone and them sitting disconsolate on the doorstep in the damp of night. It seemed that one of the other cats, the special friend of the missing one, had spent the whole evening going from window to window, looking out and making hopeless little cries.

The girls left a food dish on the step. We all went grimly off to bed. And in a hollow hour of morning — 4:40 by the bedside clock — the universe rethought its mischief. I didn't hear the small sound outside the front door. The resident authority did, though, and padding down the stairs then up again, said triumphantly, "He's back."

Tried to say it as if she'd known all along he would be. And I went to touch the shoulders of the other sleepers and convey the news, like a gift in the dark.

Headlight has not gone anywhere since his adventure. He won't even look at an open door. We would give a lot to know where and how he spent those 20-some hours, but he isn't saying. He just sleeps his days away, full of secrets.

The other cats, we noticed, did not welcome him graciously. Even his special friend hissed and spat at first. But they were only mirrors of ourselves.

Wait up in the night for a teen-ager out after curfew, staring into darkness and imagining terrible possibilities, and you may find that relief erupts in an unexpected voice when the car turns in the drive.

How alike we must be, at some primitive level of affection and of fear.

43 . A GIANT IN BED

FROM EARLIEST KITTENHOOD, Headlight surveyed the world and saw nothing and no one to be trusted. So he decided to remain a creature apart, passing his life in a state of high alert.

The older cats had mastered the art of living with humans and others of their kind. They frolicked together, cadged food, crouched on the radiator covers in winter. And, in their imaginations, stalked the rabbit that nibbled the lawn outside the window.

But Headlight was the misfit.

If a hand reached out to stroke him, he would dodge it as you'd dodge a blow. He would rest only when the others of the household were safely asleep.

He is a formidable creature. If you were to come upon him at large in the woods, you might think he'd escaped from a traveling circus. If anyone were foolish enough to try to pick him up, he would splay his paws, unsheath his knives and make himself as lovable as a bramble thicket.

If spoken to, he would withdraw to some other room. His preference, in fact, was not even to be looked at. Those other cats could take all the risks they wanted, but he meant to play it safe.

It took him a while to understand that every collision with a heavy foot was not deliberately intended, and that if you're a black cat against a black floor in a dark hall, you have some responsibility in traffic.

One day, however, he answered to his name. Another day he took the awful risk of joining someone in a chair. His own boldness horrified him. His pupils were dilated like a gunfighter's, and you could tell he regretted it immediately.

From then on, the transformation has been swift.

If he happens to be on a counter when someone passes, he reaches out a claw to catch a shirt or sweater — just to announce, in case anyone is interested, that he is there and available.

He may never tolerate being held or carried. Even now, as he's being stroked, some old memory will come to him and he'll suddenly cringe and slink away, ashamed of the docile thing he's become. Basically, I think he's right about the world. It's a dangerous place. Let your guard down, and you never know where the blow will come from. The deepest wounds result from misplaced trust.

But the solitary life — I can say from the experience of one who long ago tried it — is no bargain either. You mean to be a fighter, always on your guard. Then too many things go right and love intrudes, and without quite knowing how it happened, you lose your edge.

But in these last weeks, he seems to have found his moment and his place. His moment is the bedtime hour. His place is the bed.

There were no preliminaries. It's as if the idea came to him fully formed. One night he just appeared at the upstairs doorway, marched in as confidently as a season-ticket holder headed for his box seat, and claimed the spot between us.

Now, a regular-sized bed cat is a fine thing to have. But this one is a load. You're aware of him there, solid as a log, getting larger as the night draws on. Sometimes I wake up chilly in the darkness and find he's gathered the bedclothes to himself.

"Headlight's taken my blanket," I whine. "I am the alpha male of this house, and I don't even have a blanket to cover me."

He's looking at me, nothing but the gold coins of his eyes visible in the shine of the street lamp through the window.

"Take it back," my wife says sleepily.

But I see those eyes, enormous and unblinking. And I'm no fool.

"Poor thing," she says. "He has so little."

Morning comes eventually, and the danger passes. My authority is restored, but only temporarily. In nature, everything is temporary. The cat is changing, and I don't know where it leads.

44. CHEMISTRY

THE DAUGHTER WHO STILL is in school in another state phoned to tell us she was lonesome and needed a friendly cat. The announcement made our knees go weak.

Cats are something we do not have any shortage of. They appear out of nowhere on our doorstep. They crawl into our car in parking lots. Friends give them to us as a favor.

Cats never leave. For a little while the number remains stable, then it always goes up.

"I'm taking chemistry," she said. "I need moral support."

I agreed that anyone required to spend a summer studying chemistry deserved some kind of compensation. But it ought to be something practical like a new convertible or maybe the Hope diamond. Not a cat.

"I thought your friend's friend had one," I said.

"He does. Its name is London."

"Well, there's the solution. When you're feeling desperate, you can borrow London."

"No, the guy is leaving this month and taking his cat with him."

"Maybe we could bring you Headlight. He seems to do well in a college setting."

Headlight was one of those who came from the other school. He's gotten big as a steer, but still lacks confidence.

"It wouldn't work," she said. "He's neurotic and has low self-esteem. Headlight needs to be part of a pack."

"How's the chemistry going?" I asked her, trying to get the subject changed.

"I'm in class and lab five hours a day," she said.

"That's rough."

"Then I have to study at least six hours every night. It's all I do. I don't see anyone."

"Just hang in there."

"I will," she said. "But I really do need a cat."

She wished we'd at least think about it. And we did — for about a minute.

The telephone bulletins for the next several weeks

had to do with the Table of Elements and other fascinating stuff. I was glad to be out in the world and working for a living instead of being 20-something and memorizing facts I'd never need or want to know again.

The last call was about the final grade.

"I got a B," she said — her voice singing with elation over the wire. "The professor said I should declare a chemistry major."

"It's a miracle!" her mother and I cried out together. We are a family without scientific aptitude.

Then her voice got a hard edge to it.

"And I want a cat."

Giddy about the prodigious feat of scholarship, we must have hesitated for a heartbeat.

"It's all right, then?"

"Well . . ."

After all, the beast would be 600 miles away.

"It will be *my* cat," she promised.

"Yes, we know that."

"I'll take good care of it."

"We're sure you will," we told her. "But as loving parents, there's only one thing that bothers us just a little bit."

"What's that?" she said.

"You'll never be allowed to come home again."

THE LATER TIMES

45. THE HOMELESS

WHEREVER THE WOMEN of my household go, cats present themselves — creatures of uncommon excellence, and all of them needy. The other morning it was our older daughter telephoning from her work.

"There's this kitten," she said.

The words caused my breathing to become rapid and shallow. Our need for additional cats is not great.

"He was outside the garage where I park," she said. "It's next to a homeless shelter, and the men there have been taking care of it. It's a sweet kitty, and very friendly."

"Yes, I'm sure."

"I asked one of the men if he'd keep it until you got there."

"Until *what?*"

"He said he would. You'll know the place. You'll see a group of fellows on the sidewalk out front."

Time has taught me the uselessness of protesting. So of course I drove there, and, as promised, several men were talking together outside the doorway of the shelter. But the prize beast was nowhere to be seen, and for the briefest moment my heart leapt up.

I parked the car and approached the men. They

were chatting amiably in the cool of morning —
men of different races, but bound together by that
comradeship of people who've lost their way or lost
their luck.

"My daughter called about a cat," I said to one of
them.

"Sure," he said. "The cat. It's here somewhere."

"He wants the cat," another said.

News of my mission circulated among them.

"Where's the cat?"

"He was here a minute ago."

"It's a little tomcat," the first man said.

"I think maybe he's in the garage."

That was where they kept his food dish and his
water.

One of the men went in the garage and returned a
moment later with the cat in the crook of his arm. As
advertised, it was a handsome little fellow, about
half-grown — a gray and black tabby with fine, clear
markings and wonderfully amiable.

"Your daughter wants him, does she?"

"Well, it's really up to you," I said.

"Sure," a man said. "Take him. He needs a place."

I got the box from the car.

"You're sure you don't mind?"

"No. Go ahead."

They helped me put him in the box.

"There's some food back there if you want it."

"No," I told them. "We have some cats already. There's food at home."

I felt bad afterward about not taking it. It was what they had to give.

"I'm glad someone's going to look after that little cat," one of the men said.

"We'll get him checked out at the vet's. Get him his shots."

"Good. He's a good cat."

I put the box in the car, thanked them, and I drove away with him then — a cat who'd found his home and his luck, leaving those men standing on the sidewalk, still waiting for theirs.

46. TWO FRIENDS

THE ARRIVAL OF THE GRAY tabby kitten, Stripe, has upset the delicate equilibrium and provoked a chorus of outraged singing among the established residents.

If you've kept cats, you know that the ones with seniority never are pleased to have a newcomer among them. Ugly sounds were made. Blows were struck. Stripe, though small, was a survivor from the street, not easily daunted. But the lack of cordiality must have mystified or even saddened him a bit.

Then a strange thing happened. The striped kitten and the great black misanthrope, Headlight, found their way to each other. There's no guessing how or why, for one is feisty and combative, the other stolid and fearful, with a panther's body but a mouse's heart.

It's said sometimes that opposites attract. Or perhaps they sensed their common histories of aloneness. One day they were found sprawled close together on the couch. A day or so after that they were sleeping together in a tangle, waking from time to time for some reciprocal grooming. Stripe, being small, does not require much maintenance. But washing Headlight is an ongoing job for the little cat.

Our thought was that the kitten's lodging here would be temporary, only until our daughter could find an apartment where he'd be welcome. But now I see the plan is fatally flawed. Those two, the solitary and the newcomer, have found a meeting of the hearts that seems somehow to be a comfort against less happy times remembered.

So it's clear. Both will have to go with our daughter, or both will have to stay. In this uncertain world, a friendship like that, however improbable, is too valuable to let get away.

4 7 .   A   L I F E ' S   R E W A R D

H E NEVER FOUND governing his weight an easy matter. It's a problem with which I have some experience.

At the high-water mark, Teddy was a cat of 26 pounds. Don't just read right over that number without it registering. *Twenty-six pounds,* and all white.

The *Trophy Cat,* we called him. Visitors cried out in astonishment, swearing they'd never seen another one that big.

There must have been a point in his early life, before he came to us, when the prospect of nourishment was uncertain. He spent a lot of time looking at the food bowl. If he wasn't actually eating, he was planning to — or had just finished.

He developed a game knee, and a stool and chair in the kitchen had to be arranged in a way that allowed him to ascend to the counter by easy stages.

"You need to cut back on his ration," the veterinarian told us. And we tried. But the stuff marked *Feline Light* disgusted him, and he went directly to the bowls of the other cats.

The day he joined our household, he'd been mugged by a barn cat and had his face shaved and stitched. By any measure, that was a really bad day.

The established members of our pride took one

look and began singing their song of terror. It was no use, though, because any cat that is with us overnight is with us always.

And soon enough they discovered that inside the hugeness of him dwelt the softest of hearts. Not once, in the 13 years that followed, did I ever hear him growl. Hardly ever did he raise a paw against any of the others, and then it was only in play, claws sheathed.

His preferred sleeping place was in the old rocking chair in the living room. When he jumped up in it for the night his weight started the rockers thumping.

Time passed — on quick feet, as it has a way of doing. Cats were lost to age, but others came. Teddy was congenial toward them all.

Then, this year — his 14th we think it was, or possibly his 15th — he began seriously to fail. His weight declined to under 20 pounds, then to only a dozen. He was nimbler in his new shape, able to make it up more easily to the counter and the bowls. But he was declining all the same. He required an injection daily, which, despite our dread of needles, we trained ourselves to give.

And now, though eternally hungry, he was able to eat only a bite or two of special food at a time. And it seemed not to profit him, for when you touched him your hand could feel every bone. It wasn't our wish to keep him selfishly past his time, but he still enjoyed a few minutes outdoors on fine days, some- times making a whole circuit of the fenced back yard. And he seemed not to be experiencing pain.

The pain was in looking at him, and remembering how he'd been.

There came that recent day, though, when the eating stopped. And when for the first time he seemed unable to find a comfortable position. And when, overcome by weakness, he could move only a few steps before stopping to rest. Teddy, the Trophy Cat, may have weighed eight pounds that last day. Or maybe less.

It sometimes happens, among animals, that when a once-robust member of the pack or pride becomes disabled by age or infirmity, the others will turn on him and drive him alone into the outer darkness.

Not so with Teddy. To the very end, the other cats were tender with him — tender and respectful. They would come to press their faces against his, or to allow their tails to stroke along his back when passing.

One of them, Eric, the tuxedo cat, had been his friend from the very first. The others, when they came as kittens, were greeted and made welcome by him who, for all his great size, had such a generous nature. And now, when he needed it, they were repaying him for a lifetime of kindness.

Would that all of us could say we'd earned as much.

48. SCOOP

H E IS INQUISITIVE, aggressive, a bit thorny by nature — the ideal temperament for a reporter. What's more, he comes from a journalism background. At this point, he's only a raw talent, totally untrained — except to the litter box.

Born on Easter under a newspaperman's bed, he goes by the name of Scoop. He came to us — ear mites, worms and all — at eight weeks of age, the size, roughly, of your open hand. But he is putting on heft, 2 1/2 pounds at the latest weigh-in.

The first month he has spent quarantined in our bedroom and has not yet met the other members of the pride. The established cats sniff at the crack of the door. Their curiosity is intense.

They know he's in there. What they do not know, but are deeply concerned to learn, is just how *big* he is. A danger unseen is the worst kind. What if that brute behind the door turns out to be a cat the size of a golden retriever?

Over the years, most of Scoop's predecessors — and there've been many — have come to us half-grown or more, from the street, from farms, or through the thoughtfulness of friends and neighbors upon whose doorsteps they appeared.

For a man who never lived with a cat until he married a woman with a passion for them, and fathered daughters with the same sickness, I've not done too badly. And now, with this promising newscat, Scoop, we begin with another newcomer.

He has not yet met the bird dogs. There are three, now — Rufus's sons, Pete and Bear, and his grand-pup, Cyrus. The dogs regard the other cats, the grown ones, with fascination tempered by a healthy respect. But little Scoop is something else.

The first test, therefore, will come when we open the bedroom door and Scoop is presented to the other residents of his own kind. I expect that will be an electric moment for us all. But based on consider-able past experience, the crisis can be depended on to pass.

There'll be some ugly sounds at the start. Alliances of long standing will be rearranged. But somewhere among those others he'll find a friend. In time, he'll march among them as if he'd been here always. And they, comforted to find a cat of normal size, will have no memory of the days before he came.

Hearts, like houses, can expand to make room for as many as need a place.

49 . THE GAMER

IMAGINATION IS BOTH a gift and a curse of being human.

It is a key element of foresight, enabling us to envision a range of possible outcomes and base our action on a balance of risks and benefits we can surmise, but not surely know.

At the same time, imagination is at the root of a disability that nearly all of us share in some measure: the fear of failure.

Many workers remain in jobs they find tedious and unrewarding because they can imagine how a more challenging occupation might defeat them.

Casualties of a broken marriage often shun new relationships out of fear they might fail again.

Writers can be blocked from beginning the next project by the dread that it could turn out less well than the last one.

Nowhere is this handicap — or the lack of it — more apparent than in the world of sport. There are, among athletes, ones with a reputation as "gamers." They are the Michael Jordans and the John Elways who, when their team is trailing in the biggest contest of the year and the final seconds are ticking off the clock, want the ball in their hands.

They want that last shot, that last chance at the

end zone. It simply does not occur to them that they might fail. And even if sometimes they do, the thought of it does not cross their minds in the moment. Ones like that are supremely rare, which is why, in professional sport, they get the big money.

My boyhood athletic career was, to be charitable about it, undistinguished. I was small and slow afoot, but those were not my chief handicaps. During practice, or when not much was at stake, I could display acceptable skills. But when it counted, imagination disabled me.

In the same way that some are able to fix their minds on images of success, I would find myself considering the vast range of possibilities for humiliating failure. Thus my talents, modest as they were, diminished in direct proportion to the gravity of the moment. I just was not a gamer, and despised this defect in myself as much as I envied those lucky ones who seemed free of it.

What brought this to mind was a little squeak of terror I heard my wife utter a few moments ago from an upper region of the house.

"Are you hurt?" I called up to her.

"No," she replied. "It's Tommy. He's on the banister again."

Tommy is one of the newer members of our tribe — a sweet-natured, faintly marked gray tabby whom we saw at a pet supply store adoption day, and brought home to be a kitten friend for Scoop. He came to us distinctly bowlegged, a bit clumsy. And, maturing, he has put on some weight. You'd never take him for a player, much less a gamer. But he has gotten this astonishing habit of perching on the second-floor railing of the stair.

Never mind if the early morning or late evening light is uncertain. He'll be running along the upstairs hall and suddenly, without breaking stride, he will bound up onto the banister which measures only two inches and a fraction wide. And there he will squat like a plump gray hen, perfectly at ease, with nothing but air between him and the hardwood floor 15 feet below.

It is unnerving to see, and worries us a good deal. But Tommy, unencumbered by fear, does this thing as easily as you or I might pass from one room to another, never even considering the possibility of a bad result.

More than a few athletes, I suspect, would give everything to play the game that way. Because raw physical gifts — size and strength and uncommon agility — are helpful if you happen to have them. But more than anything, it's that inability to imagine failure that separates the merely competent from those who make it to the Hall of Fame.

50. SURVIVAL'S WAY

WITH ONLY THE GLASS between them, faces not an inch apart, Tommy and the bird dog Bear examine one another through the lower pane of the door. Their expressions are civil, but powerfully curious.

Bear respects and admires cats. He is impressed by their ability to levitate in an eye blink from floor to kitchen countertop, where they can snack at will from their food bowls he cannot reach.

He has learned, from hard experience, exactly how close he is permitted to pass by the irascible calico one, Spanky, without provoking a spectacular and sometimes painful demonstration.

Grown cats he understands. But smaller ones are new in his experience. What Tommy, and his colleague, Scoop, know of dogs is only that they are presences that dwell on the other side of the glass.

At night, before the pups come in, the kittens are sequestered in their private room. A moment later they hear a joyful clamor on the stair. Released in the morning, they tour our bedroom, sniffing the chair and rug where Bear, Pete and Cyrus have slept. And they are puzzled, I think, by how the scent got there, since they've seen no dogs except the ones who live in the yard.

Why keep them apart at all?

The three pups, though birds are their profession, also are fierce with squirrels. A kitten — especially a gray one like Tommy — is of a size to be confused with those impudent things that climb the trees and walk the wires. We did not want to take a chance that, in the excitement of the first close meeting, one of the pups might make a mistake.

All dogs, it is said, genetically are wolves, and cats must all be lions of a sort — two species separated by an evolutionary abyss. Yet I'm struck by how much the delicate protocols of this mixed household are like those of the larger world, even among all us creatures with opposable thumbs.

The different tribes of us — the tribes of America, no less than those of Africa, Asia and the tortured Middle East — peer at one another as if through a glass darkly. We see differences, of appearance or creed or habit, and make much of those. What we note less clearly, if at all, are the commonalities — the vastly broader ground of shared dreams and fears and needs. And thus we remain, in many ways, strangers to one another's lives.

Tommy and Scoop have grown now beyond first kittenhood, and are unmistakably cats, if still small-ish ones. The time is at hand when they and the pups must learn to live without the glass between them. And they will. There may be a tricky moment or two at first, but they will find an accommodation, for the simple reason that they have no choice.

This household and all who abide here — wolves and lions and higher (or lower) mammals all together — are their universe, the only one they'll ever know.

And in a closed universe, theirs or ours, tolerance is survival's way.

5 1 . T R A N S P L A N T E D

THE OLDER DAUGHTER has taken a new apartment, and though we will miss her company the progression is the expected one. They grow up. They leave. It's perfectly natural. But two of the cats have gone with her, and that is *not* natural at all. Cats come. Cats stay.

Stripe, the agile youngster from the street, is reported to have taken nicely to his new lodgings — exploring closets, elevating to the tops of things, sleeping days and bouncing off the walls at night.

But with the other one, the introvert Headlight, it's a different matter. It took him six years to decide a hand reaching down to stroke him was not a mortal threat. He still cannot be held. And he cherishes routine. Any rearrangement of feeding stations always filled him with profound concern.

Then came Stripe, whose rowdy fearlessness

aroused in old Headlight a faint recollection of kittenhood — of how things may once have been, and
might yet be. And they became immediate friends.

The big one let himself be deviled without com-
plaint. He was pounced on from atop chairs,
ambushed at the corner of the hall. And into the cold
shine of those yellow eyes there came a softening,
something like affection. When Stripe tired of mischief, they napped together on the couch, their arms
flung companionably over each other.

It was understood from the start that the kitten
would move with his mistress. But to separate
Headlight from his life's one friend? Unthinkable! So
they went together to the new apartment, and now the
problem. Great, timid Headlight has not adjusted well.

The first day and night he spent under the bed,
crying out in desolation. The second night he hid
behind the bathtub, declining nourishment. The
third day he was glimpsed briefly, and was persuaded to take a few bites of tuna.

These bulletins of his slight progress, received by
phone, were not encouraging. What's more, we *missed*
him. Reclusive though he'd always been, he was a
part of our tribe.

My wife got out the cat carrier and set it by the
door, in readiness to bring him home. But then the
news improved. He had begun moving about the

new place — had been spied on the window ledge and on the back of the couch, showing moderate interest in the world outside the glass. Then he crept to the bed at night. Not for the whole night — only a timid hour. But that was a start.

Yesterday, finally, there came the word we'd hoped for. Our daughter, returning in the evening from her work, found the two of them nestled together on the coverlet, arms across each other as had always been their habit.

So it's settled now. The cat carrier has gone back to the basement. And Headlight has discovered a saving truth.

Change may come, unannounced and unexplained, to dismantle the world you knew. But even in those most dangerous of times, one friend can get you through.

52. CYRUS REMEMBERS

THE BRITTANY BIRD DOG, Cyrus, a fine example of the breed, will be 4 years old in June. He weighs in at a bit over 45 pounds.

His father and his uncle are 8, coming 9 in May. And as middle age and the hurts of a sporting life have slowed them, Cyrus has become the alpha dog. The other two defer graciously, accepting the reality of pack politics. They know the torch has passed.

He's not mean about it. But he does insist on his right to pass first through doorways and, in the evening, to claim his preferred bedroom chair for sleeping.

In the field he's a tireless worker, unintimidated by other dogs. In fact, as far as we know, in all the world there is only one thing Cyrus fears.

The gray cat, Tommy, is a bit older than Cyrus. He came to us as a kitten, and has never known a day's discomfort. But for reasons unknown, he has spent his years afraid of nearly everything — a sudden noise, a sharp word, an abrupt movement.

Yet it is this Tommy, weighing just over 11 pounds — small and soft and with timidest of natures — who is the single unspeakable terror in Cyrus's life.

It is possible to date, to the exact instant, the event that shaped their relationship.

Cyrus, a woolly, rowdy pup of eight or nine weeks, was new in the house, following his nose and exploring every corner. Poor Tommy, undone by all this commotion, had taken refuge under the bed for a little peace.

Inevitably, of course, the pup's nose led him there. He thrust his face close to the dust-ruffle, and that's when Tommy came out like a projectile from a cannon — not in aggression but in pure fright, all noise and swollen tail.

The pup withdrew, with three undignified backward somersaults that took him halfway across the room. It was his very first acquaintance with the truth that life does not always show a welcoming face.

Years now have passed since that defining moment. Cyrus has come to know that all cats are not alike. Most, in fact, are reasonably placid creatures.

Tommy, for his part, seems to have forgotten the encounter. Dogs, to him, are just presences to be largely ignored, and he moves among them as indifferent to Cyrus as to the others.

Cyrus, however, is far from indifferent. His sense of Tommy is set in stone.

When the gray cat enters the room, Cyrus becomes rigid as a statue. He hardly breathes, and his eyes, showing much white, follow Tommy's every move.

Touch him, and you will feel him trembling under your hand.

It's pitiful to see — that powerful alpha dog so transfixed and immobilized by fear of a creature that, alongside him, would hardly look to be more than a mouthful. (Though we try not to think of it in those terms.)

It must be that, with dogs as with people, some of life's first wounds leave memories that never heal.

53. ELUSIVE ORDER

THE KITCHEN DRAWER IN which Scoop's things are kept is too high for him to reach. By standing atop a box, however, and stretching to his full height, he was able to open the drawer and select his favorite toy, the fuzzy orange ball.

This accomplishment, and the obvious act of reasoning that directed it, would not have been particularly noteworthy in a child — even a small and fairly limited child. But Scoop isn't a child. He's a cat, a black one, born under a newspaperman's bed and heir to all the unfortunate habits of poking and prying that go with the journalist's trade.

While Scoop was opening the drawer and rifling through its contents, Tommy was busy in what my wife calls his office. This "office" is a cabinet in the breakfast room, where towels, napkins, place mats and folded sheets are kept. The sheets are for covering car seats while transporting furred members of the household to their various appointments.

The cabinet's doors latch when closed, but Tommy has solved the latch. Each day, faithful as any clerk punching the clock, he opens his office and drags out the sheets. His purpose in doing it is not obvious, but he would not dream of letting a day go by without tending to this important work.

And then there is the new kitten — yes, *another one!* She was found in a mechanic's garage, just down the street from the veterinarian who cares for our menagerie. She still is unnamed.

That's because she's a transient, bound at month's end for a more cosmopolitan life. She'll be a New Yorker, and her business there will be to entertain and console a young woman, our daughter, filling in as best she can the empty place left by the loss of a beloved cat — the one who'd gotten our daughter through the ordeal of college chemistry.

But in the meantime she lodges with us. We isolated her in a room of her own, but she objected, shoving objects under the door to petition for freedom.

Yesterday morning, sitting at the breakfast room table with the newspaper and my first coffee, I heard a whine and looked up to see the orange-and-white bird dog, Pete, wearing an expression of profound sorrow. The new kitten, released from confinement, had marched directly up and sniffed the various parts of him, frightening the great hunter almost witless.

Behind me, I could hear Tommy in his office, dragging out sheets.

Scoop was up on his box, feeling with one arm over the rim of the drawer.

Now the smallest one of all was abusing the dog.

And in that somber early hour it was revealed clearly to me, if I'd ever doubted it, that any hope of order in this crowded life of ours had long ago been lost.

54. SPANKY

SPANKY, THE CAT WHO never liked cats, is reaping the harvest of a lifetime's bad temper. She passes her days, now, frowning out at the world from the seat of one or another of the chairs that circle the breakfast room table.

Her food bowl is in a room just off the kitchen, and she must creep back there secretly at night to take nourishment while the rest of the household is sleeping.

If she tries to make that journey by daylight, the other cats converge to devil her, and she has to scuttle along, hissing and sputtering with humiliation, while they trail behind, batting at her flanks.

She's a pretty creature, and vain — black and brown and white, with a pink nose and the largest gold-green eyes you ever saw in the face of a cat. She likes people, and always has. Dogs she dominates with a level stare, letting them know from the start that she's not to be fooled with. It's only other cats she truly despises.

For 10 years, at least, she ruled her kingdom from the landing of the stairs, perched like a smug hen, but prowling out from there wherever and whenever it pleased her to. She was slender then, and agile as any of the others. They allowed her to pass unmolested, giving her the respect she demanded, to which she was entitled by seniority.

Then, just in recent months, her spirit could be seen to falter. Maybe age and the inevitable thickening of her middle accounted for it. That can happen with the aging beauties of any species when they begin to notice the changes in themselves. Or maybe she saw something in the eyes of the younger ones, grown now to the fullness of their powers — some subtle difference in the way those others regarded her.

Whatever the explanation, her confidence, her sense of herself and of her place in the world, deserted her. She took sanctuary under the breakfast table. And except when she slips out from there at night, that chair seat now is her world.

We try to speak to her, and to stroke her in passing when we think to do it. She purrs noisily with gratitude for being noticed. It is what she has these days in the way of a social life. The other cats make a deliberate point of walking close by her chair, or they stand on the table and lower a paw over the edge to announce their nearness. Her growl of alarm and indignation can be heard all through the house.

True, there are certain small compensations. She is strategically positioned to observe much of the activity of the house. And for a good part of the day, bright sun-light streams through the window to warm her chair.

Still, it's a lonely life she has made for herself. The trouble is those other cats have not forgotten how things *used* to be. Isn't that the way it often goes when the powerful fall?

55 . OFF BY A WEEK

IT HAS BEEN OUR RULE, when on vacation, never to count away the days — just spend them easily, and let the end come as a surprise. Otherwise, there's sad-ness from the very start.

Now, with daughters grown and occupied with lives of their own, occasions as a family all together are harder to come by, and the rule about ignoring time's brevity is even more important.

For part of this week, the daughter working in New York will be home for the holiday, and her sis-ter has tickets for the two of them to some raucous musical event. One day, if the weather allows, we'll go to the country and pass a few hours fishing and grazing in the blackberry patch. Part of another — the holiday itself — we'll spend with friends. Beyond that, not much is planned.

Mostly, I think, we will just want to talk. It isn't that we've been out of touch. We have quite regular telephone conversations, but, as anyone knows, those are somehow not entirely real, or at any rate do not suffice.

The problem simply is one of distance. I know people whose children have scattered like thistledown to the farthest corners of this country and even of the planet. And I'm sure there are fine adventures to be found there. But I'm uneasy with that. Something in me despises separation.

Planes fly, those people say. And it's true. But one is too seldom on them.

Above all, we'll want to hear the latest news about her new family. In a matter of only months, she has gone from being a young woman alone in a fifth-floor walk-up to being the matriarch and sole caretaker of a gang of seven.

First she was joined by the gray tabby kitten, Zipper, the little female found in the mechanic's garage. Then came Valentine, also only weeks old, gotten from a shelter as company for Zip. Naturally it was essential for Valentine, who was male, to be neutered as soon as he was of an age for it. In certain matters, paying close attention to time is essential. But sometimes, as the song says, *time just gets away.*

Valentine had his surgery all right. Taking into consideration the 62- to 63-day gestation period of cats, and counting backward, his surgery was about one week too late. So, despite her relative youth and small size, Zipper was delivered of five surprises. By sheer luck, it happened when the mistress of the apartment was there to witness the birthing, which she managed to do without fainting.

Zip is reported to be a good mother and Valentine an interested father, though somewhat baffled as new fathers usually are. All are reported doing well. The kittens' eyes are just opening. And already all but one are spoken for, meaning that they will not become public charges of the city of New York.

This we've been told over the telephone, but that's what I mean by phone calls being inadequate. We've been impatient for our daughter's visit, and of course we're eager to see her for herself.

But more than that, like any grandparents, we can't wait to see the pictures.

56. SLEEP NO MORE

THE DAYS ARE LONG this time of year. And the nights are short — not just the hours of darkness, but the hours for sleeping.

Sometime after 2:30 a.m., never later than 4, the bird dogs begin to stir. I hear the jingle of Pete's collar as he jumps down from the chair that I would have liked to sit in the evening before, if he had not gotten to it first.

That bit of activity wakes Bear, who has napped at the far end of the room in the other chair, the one we fatuously speak of as my wife's. Then Bear's son, Cyrus, joins them — all shaking their collars, toenails clicking on the wood floor, and Pete, the vocal one, making porcine little squeals.

"*Be quiet!*" I tell them, sometimes embellishing the command with a curse. "*Get back in your chairs. I mean, our chairs.*"

There is blessed silence, which lasts, on average, about three or four minutes. Then the jingling, clicking racket is repeated, Pete's squeals expand into bleats and yowls. So I bound from bed and, trying not to let them trip me on the stair, descend to let them out into the fenced back yard.

When I return to the bed, I find the gray cat, Tommy, is in my place. But, folding myself around him, I manage to lie down. Sweet sleep returns. I dream.

In the dream I am running through a dark wood, pursued by something large and dangerous. I hear the scratching of its awful claws on the path behind. The sound is closer. Then closer still — and terrifying.

It is another of the cats, scratching at the door, wanting in where it is cool.

Ours may be the only house south of Skagway without central air conditioning. Certainly it is the only one on our block. Individual window units create small islands of comfort, and we move hastily between them, sensing vaguely that there might be a better way to live.

Mostly our primitive existence is a matter of no importance to the cats. But in middle summer, when the swollen sun sets the world afire, they are reminded again of how cruelly they're disadvantaged. So they demonstrate.

Through the window I see a spotlight pass by on the street below. It is the van of the man who delivers the newspaper — the first announcement of morning although the sky still shows no creeping sign of dawn.

More scratching at the door. This time it's Eric, the tuxedo cat, who has decided that further malingering cannot be allowed. He brings his face very close, and moving it from side to side with deliberate malice, he *whiskers* the would-be sleepers to their feet.

That is what passes for a night of sleep.

Just a moment ago, I nodded off while sitting here and trying to write. That happens often. I say *a moment ago*, but actually I don't know how long it's been.

Outside it is full light, now. Neighborhood men are leaving to their work. The dogs, having slumbered half the night in chairs and the other half in the dew-cool grass, are fully rested and ready for their day. The cats, who are reported to sleep 18 hours of every 24, have eaten, groomed themselves, and are settling down for their next six.

By my best calculation, my hours of actually uninterrupted rest have totaled four — about normal as nights go.

Which is why I consider myself lucky to have managed to hang on all these years in the journalist's trade, rather than getting in a line of work that required me to spend my days disarming bombs or operating dangerous machinery.

One can keep animals, or hold down some kind of responsible occupation, but one can't do both.

57. CRAZY IN N.Y.

WE ARE VISITING OUR New York daughter, and it is half-past 3 o'clock in the morning. In the apartment directly below, occupied by three Argentine rock musicians, the party still is going hard.

I sit on the edge of the bed, because if I lie down the *ka-whunk* of the electric bass comes up through the floor, into the legs of the bed and through the pillow to my ear. It's like being at the party, but with nothing to drink.

So I sit on the bed and look through the window at the shine of a streetlight along the empty Brooklyn street and am toying with the idea of committing an antisocial act. From time to time, the daughter's black cat, Valentine, comes to stand in the bedroom door and look at me sitting on the bed.

Valentine rarely permits himself to be seen by day. He lives under the futon or in the springs of the bed. When he is feeling exceptionally nervous he goes behind the kitchen stove and hides somewhere in the workings of the gas oven.

New York can get you crazy that way.

The daughter hasn't used the stove in months for fear of incinerating the cat. So there's nothing in the refrigerator. She gets carry-out from the deli instead, or cooks in the microwave. But the kitchen is small. The only place to put the microwave is on top of the empty refrigerator, and there are only so many dishes one can prepare while cooking at a level two feet above one's head.

Probably if she ate in, instead of spending a fortune on carry-out, she would be able to afford a place with a modern stove that a cat couldn't get inside, and quiet neighbors on the next floor down. But here, in order to eat, she'd have to risk cooking Valentine, so it is a vicious circle.

At 4 o'clock the party moves from the first floor of

the building into the street, which I take for a sign that the affair may be winding down. As nearly as I can tell, they have been playing the same song — at least the beat is the same — for six and a half hours without interruption

*   *   *   *

That was last night.

Today, my wife and daughter, who slept through the party were rested and refreshed. Valentine and I are frazzled. If there were room for me inside the stove, I would go in there with him.

We took a bus and a train into Manhattan for breakfast, then spent a couple of hours at a museum, had a light lunch in the museum cafeteria, and stopped to watch the dogs and their owners at one of the fenced dog walks New Yorkers have in their public parks.

It was getting well on in the day when we came back to Brooklyn.

Hassidic men, perspiring in fur hats and black frock coats on a day in the 80s, were passing self-contained and mysterious along the sidewalks of the neighborhood. And on the stoop outside the apartment on the building's bottom floor the Argentine musicians — fresh as new daisies — were just then having their breakfast. Orange juice and toast, in the middle of afternoon.

"They're students at Juilliard," said our daughter.

"You don't say."

They looked like nice enough young men, but I was uninterested in their educational careers. It was their plans for later that worried me. I am not a swinging New Yorker. I am a man of regular habits, with a tidy little life, and there's no telling what could happen if I have to spend another night sitting on the edge of the bed.

Sure enough, just as I lay down, I heard a preliminary *ka-whunk* of the electric bass warming up.

"We're in for it," I told Valentine the cat — wherever he happened to be.

But it was a false alarm. Somebody had knocked over a trash can down on the street.

New York can get you crazy that way.

58 . QUICK HANDS

L IKE ANY MEMBER OF the journalistic tribe, Scoop never passes up a chance at food.

It's well known, among people in our trade, that if you invite colleagues to drop around for a party, you'd better double the order for whatever you're serving. As a rule, the locusts won't make off with the silver. But it pays to lock up anything in the house you don't want eaten or drunk.

Scoop comes out of that tradition, and if you forget it even for a moment he will, as they say, eat your lunch.

He's a lean, somewhat spidery creature. We all were lean once, though I could tell him from experience that will change. He also is amazingly agile, and has uncommonly long arms — the famous boarding-house reach.

Say there is some especially delectable morsel that you have kept in the refrigerator for a couple of days as a test of character, an exercise in deferred satisfaction. Finally you come to the considered judgment that the proper moment has arrived. You open the refrigerator, remove the saved delight and turn aside for a moment to get a fork from the drawer of flatware.

Bad mistake!

Turning back to pick up the saucer, you find the morsel gone. Scoop has materialized from nowhere, and is looking at you levelly, without remorse.

Or you pass the kitchen counter with a freshly made sandwich on a plate. You are a moving target and thus, you would imagine, safe. But arriving at the table, you discover your planned snack has been reduced by half.

He is gifted. And he is very, very fast. The only talent I've ever seen in a class with his was among the

Gypsy pickpockets of Paris, with whom we became well-acquainted in the year we lived there.

One of them took a 200-franc bill — about $20 — from my wife's hand in a museum line, and did it with such dexterity that by the time she knew she'd been hit, the thief was vaulting a wall and disappearing along the quay of the Seine.

Another explored my coat pockets during a ride in a crowded Metro car. I remember glancing at him. He was a striking character — swarthy face sharp as a hawk's, with a thick scar down one cheek. He ignored me, staring straight ahead, though his clever hand was busy all the time. And at the next stop, in the last instant before the door closed, he darted out and away, having only taken a small notebook instead of my wallet by mistake.

After some months I was alert to them and the way they worked, often in pairs or threes, and spent a whole day following a group of them, watching them relieve tourists of their goods. At midday, they repaired to a fast-food place to buy burgers and milk-shakes from the morning take. They worked hard. And, regardless of what you might think of it, you have to admire anyone who's that good at a trade.

That's how I feel about Scoop. But there's an important difference.

We always knew that, when winter came and the

raw winds blew in from the Channel or down from the North Sea, the pickpockets would load their caravans and migrate southward from Paris to some warmer place. Or our year there would end, and we would leave.

But Scoop's not going anywhere. And neither are we. We're all in this together, for the duration. So it looks like a food fight to the finish.

59. A MELLOWING

THE CALICO CAT, Spanky, has had a personality change — she has become softer of nature, more affectionate.

In her earlier years she was a dour creature, crabbed and secretive by temperament, frowning out at the world with an owlish glare. It was the other cats she especially despised. Some find this distaste for one's own species baffling, but I have to say I understand completely. There are a fair number of human beings for which I have no use.

After a time, she shifted her station from the stair landing to the seat of a breakfast-room chair. And finally to a back room off the kitchen, where she passed her days in solitude.

But then this remarkable change occurred. It didn't happen gradually. It came almost overnight, as if she'd simply decided, after long observation and much consideration, that life was sweeter for those who made the effort to be sociable.

So she awoke one morning a beast of an entirely different sort.

She has been seen deliberately approaching the other cats of the household, though the terror of those others, the first time that happened, was very great. She joins them on the kitchen counter for the distribution of bits of leftover chicken or fish.

From time to time, in past years, I found it necessary to extract a shed claw, hers, from the muzzle of one or the other of the pups. She has not yet established anything that could be described as a friendship with them. It's more a guarded accommodation. But at least now the dogs are able to pass up and down the stairs freely and are not transfixed by dread if she happens to come in the room.

And what's the result of all this congeniality?

Well, Spanky has discovered the comfort of couch and upstairs bed, and sleeps now in softer places. And, as the others yield to her surprising overtures, she receives their companionship. And shares the little treats that they have long enjoyed. And being so much easier to live with, she naturally receives more stroking and hears her extraordinary beauty more often commented upon.

The change, in other words, has paid off handsomely.

I wait to see in myself any of this softening of a prickly nature that the greater wisdom of age is rumored to bring, but I do not detect it yet. They say such amazing transformations sometimes occur in violent and predatory criminals, who are then able to put a life of unspeakable behavior behind and go forth, hold tent revivals, give motivational seminars, appear on daytime talk shows and otherwise serve their fellow man.

I have no great faith in that, either, though it's a pretty notion. In Spanky, the change cannot be doubted. But cats, by and large, are better than the rest of us.

60. HIS GOLD CORDS

SCOOP UNDERSTANDS, as all of us do, that life is a precarious business and order is everything. A little carelessness or inattention, and everything gets away. So he is careful with his belongings, the most precious of which are his gold cords.

His toy mice also are nice, but it's the gold cords that he values above all else. We're not altogether sure of their origins. They were gotten long ago, before Scoop's time, perhaps for wrapping gifts or as Christmas decorations.

Among his talents is the ability to open drawers. So he opened one, spied the cords rolled up in a ball, unrolled it and took them out. There are five — four about six feet long and one a bit shorter, all roughly half the thickness of a clothesline rope.

Scoop is an imposing cat, pure glossy black with half-inch saber claws he keeps considerately hidden. It is surprising to see in so formidable a beast such devotion to those cords and to the game we play with them.

I will be passing through a room and he will fling himself down on the carpet, then inch along on his side to indicate his readiness for a little sport. And I will go to find one of the gold cords.

There's never any mystery about where to look. He keeps them in the back room, where the food bowls now are located. Lust was surgically eliminated, leaving food and the cords as his central concerns. It reassures him, I believe, to have both in one place. Most generally, the end of one or more of the cords actually is *in* the food bowl, although often the fifth may be found in the kitchen, in the bowl of water, which he also considers important.

Sometimes he follows me on my errand, but usually, when I come back with the cord, he is waiting, drawn tight as a violin string with eagerness and excitement.

It is a stalking, hunting, catching game we play. I hold one end of the cord and back away so that the length of it is stretched on the floor. At a range of 10 feet or so, he flattens himself on the carpet beside a chair, or on the hall stair.

His chin is low, his eyes fixed, his ears laid back to reduce his profile. If it is late evening or early morning, he chooses a shadowed place where he can be less clearly seen. I jiggle the cord, and the end of it twitches. There is an almost imperceptible tensing of his haunches. He is an arrow drawn and aimed. I jiggle the cord again.

And so swiftly the eye scarcely can record it, *the arrow flies!*

His gift at the thing he was born to do is wonderful to see. Always in that moment I experience a little thrill of gratitude that I am my size and he is his, and that I am not a mouse.

He does not catch his prey on every charge. Sometimes I pluck the cord away in time. But invariably that is how the game finally ends. I congratulate him. The seized end of the cord is clamped securely in his teeth. The rest of it I fling over and around him — across his forehead and ears, down his back and around his tail.

"Much decorated cat," I cry out in praise. *"Mentioned in dispatches."*

And he walks away, the end of the cord trailing behind — his head held high, marching proudly, like some very senior commander whose rank is signaled by an abundance of gold braid.

Scoop, the newspaper cat, would no more dream of being careless with the equipment than a responsible reporter would be careless about the saving of his notes. So straight through the kitchen he goes, and around the corner into the back room to put his cord in his food bowl, and perhaps take a little nourishment while he's there.

61. REACHING OUT

WE LOST SPANKY this month.

A dozen years ago, a runty, ratty kitten had reached out its paw through the wire of a shelter cage to a girl passing by. And, by that one small gesture, had found its place in the world.

The girl was a student in the college in that town, more than a thousand miles — a lonely distance — away from home. The kitten went back to the dormitory to be the girl's friend.

There's no explaining how so unpromising a creature managed to grow into a great beauty. It's just one of those mysterious things that sometimes happens, with cats as with people. Look at the early girlhood photos of Julia Roberts if you don't believe it.

The little cat was smooth-haired, tricolored, with huge eyes and a distinctive brown spot in the green iris of the left one.

Some later time the girl came home for a holiday visit. And as frequently is the case with college cats, instead of going back to school she joined the household of the girl's parents.

It was not an easy merger. Already many lives were assembled there: one old dog, a rescue from the street; one rowdy bird dog youngster and many established cats. Exactly what number of them I prefer not to say. Five? Eight? The count is fluid, ever changing. Certainly fewer than 10.

Spanky, it turned out, was fond of people, but barely tolerated dogs and didn't care at all for other cats. She lived a life apart.

For most of her 12 years, that's simply how it was. We had tried to entice her back into the world from which she'd inexplicably withdrawn, but with very little success.

Then, one sweet late-summer day, we discovered her lounging perfectly at ease in a patch of sunlight on a little carpet in the kitchen. Nothing of the old fury was in her, nor any of the later fears. For whatever reason, her nature had abruptly changed.

Sensing the difference, the other cats came close around her, touching noses. One of them pressed the side of his face against hers, and she seemed pleased by their company.

Not long after that, cancer claimed her. Mercifully

there was no long agony, no protracted wasting. The end was swift.

I don't know if she'd had an intimation of things ending, as some believe that animals do. I'd rather think she had simply arrived at last at a state of peace with the universe of which she was a part, a sureness of her own belonging.

Whatever the explanation, she ended her days in the same way she had begun — not alone, but reaching out. Surely for any of us that's the better choice.

6 2 . A M Y S T E R Y C A T

THE NEW YORK DAUGHTER was home for a short visit — too short. We fished a bit. Ate well. Saw some movies. Then she flew back to Gomorrah, and telephoned us when she got there.

Her voice was electric with alarm and wonder.

"There's an extra cat here!" she said.

"There's a *what?*"

Cats are drawn to us. I don't know what it is — something about our odor, maybe — but they are drawn as if by an irresistible force.

That daughter has three deliberate cats, as does her sister. But she'd returned to a fourth one.

The event was unprecedented. Except by the biological process of multiplication, who ever has heard of the number of cats in an apartment increasing while the occupant was away?

"I saw it out of the corner of my eye," she said. "For a second I thought it was Zip" — that being the name of her cat No. 1. "Then I noticed it had white feet. I tried to catch it, but it ran behind the stove."

"And . . .?"

"It's still there."

"Is it?" I said. "Well, don't use the oven. And keep us informed — occasionally."

I try to be as noncommittal as possible where found cats are concerned, always alert to the danger that they might end up being transported — across miles or even whole continents — to end up sleeping in my bed. It has occurred before, more than once.

"I believe I know what happened," she said. "There were some men working in the building. I'm guessing they saw this cat and decided it probably was one of mine. So they just opened the door and put it in."

I said nothing.

"What do you think?" she asked.

"I think you need to take that up with the work-men," I told her.

Then, another day: "I've had the cat at the vet's. He says it's a girl. She's had all the tests and she's healthy."

"That's nice."

"The vet says she must have been somebody's pet.

She's very gentle. She likes being held."

Again, I said nothing.

"I'm making signs to put up in the neighborhood."

"Yes," I said. "By all means. Put up signs."

That wasn't the end of it. The bulletins have kept coming, almost daily.

"I haven't had any calls yet."

"I see."

"Three people have torn my phone number off the signs."

"You want to be careful about that," I told her. "We advertised a found cat once, and your mother got a call while I was at work. He was a heavy breather. And when she hung up on him he called back mad."

"Well, nobody's called," she said.

"So where's the beast now?"

"Shut up in the bathroom. She has food and water and a litter box in there. But she's frightened, and I don't want to integrate her with the others."

"Probably not."

"What if there aren't any calls at all?"

One would think that the 1,232 highway miles between Kansas City and New York might provide some margin of safety. But I could see where the conversation was headed.

Don't misunderstand. I like cats. I like them a lot. For the first half of my life I was strictly a dog man, then I married a cat woman. I was infected by her, and the cats began coming to our door.

(You may not believe this. But even as I was writing the previous paragraph an acquaintance called, asking if we might have a place in our herd for a rescued and somewhat disabled cat.)

"If I can't find somebody to take her," my daughter said, "I might have to put her on a plane."

"A plane to where?"

"You *know* where."

And she was right. I did know where.

"Don't even joke about it," I told her. "Make more signs."

"I am," she said.

And that's where we left it, for now. But a sense of great danger hangs over me.

63. MET ON THE TRAIL

THE DAY WAS ONE OF those autumn gifts you sometimes get, with the sky washed clean, a light breeze warming, the sweet sun sparkling on the leaf litter of the season.

I'd gone to the country on some necessary errand. And with that business finished, still had a part of the afternoon to loiter. So, instead of turning home along the highway, I took the side road that winds up into the hills to that corner of the woods where, in the best parts of the year, my heart lives.

The gate was chained, as I'd left it. And the cabin had been untouched by the season's fires. The roof needs fixing where it has begun to leak a bit at the comb, but the stain on the inner ceiling was not noticeably bigger. And except for a trespassing mouse, there was no sign of any intrusion.

The mouse's needs are small, his predations bearable. Any food left on the shelves is in tins or jars. He gnaws a little newspaper for a nest. One year he found a tube of toothpaste, and tasted that — exhaling foamy bubbles, I imagine, and leaving tiny, wonderfully delicate white footprints.

That mouse, or someone of his generations, has lived there always. When the next spring comes, he'll be out and gone to some burrow among the stones. At first frost, he'll be back again. Every woods cabin has one. And mine is a well-mannered lodger. He doesn't colonize, only borrows.

I had brought a couple of pictures to hang, photographs from an earlier hunt. So I added those to the gallery on the wall, made a last check about, then snapped closed the padlock on the door. But still there was no hurry to leave. The air was shirt-sleeve mild. And, behind the cabin, the lane bent away invitingly through the trees down toward the pond.

With the oaks bare of leaves, the pine trees plant-
ed more than 20 years ago stood out clearly, grown
straight and slender from their reaching for the light.
The trunk of one was barkless on the side where a
buck deer had rubbed his antlers. Beyond that one
was another, then another — defining the creature's
habitual line of march.

Ahead, between the trees, was the glitter of the
pond.

Just as the lane made its last turn, I was startled to
notice at a distance of maybe 50 steps something
white lying among the leaves in one of the wheel
tracks. A piece of cloth, I guessed it was, or a wadded
paper.

Coming closer, I realized it was something alive —
or once alive. I saw it was a cat. But how had a white
cat gotten flattened there on my lane where for
months no car had passed? I took another step. Its
head swung round, and two bright eyes skewered me.

*Who was this man-creature who'd come blundering heavy-
footed to spoil the year's first hunt? And why was he stopping
now? What were his intentions?*

I would have crouched to put out a friendly hand, or
at least to speak a word or two. But as the thought was
forming, and before it could be acted on, the cat sprang
up from its leaf nest — *erupted* from it, really — and with

a furrowed scowl, not so much alarmed as vexed, shot past me and was gone back up the lane in a single fluid glide, sudden as light giving way to shadow.

Pure white cats are splendid and somehow magical travelers in this world. I can date several of the most important passages of my life by their comings and goings. To happen on one accidentally, in an autumn woods where no cat of any kind belongs or ever has been seen, is more than common luck. It's an omen of a season well begun, rich with the promise of other fine and unexpected things.

64 . HAPPY'S CHANCE

TWO WEEKS PASSED. Maybe more. The wind blew down from the north and the nights grew sharper. There was a powerful intimation of winter soon to come.

We spoke about the white cat I'd seen on the pond path. We spoke about it quite a bit, in fact.

"Was it all white?" my wife asked.

"I think so. It was awfully dirty but, yes, I think all white."

"Boy or girl?"

"No way to know. It didn't let me near."

"Do you suppose it has a home?"

Just her asking the question made duty inescapable, and that weekend I made the 100-mile drive to the cabin. A pointless errand, I thought, as I turned in the drive.

But there he — or she — was, crouched by the opening at the side of the cabin, the den where over the years a coyote, a couple of foxes and at least one stray dog had born their careless litters and nursed their young.

Still filthy, hardly bigger than a ferret and no doubt hungry, it fled through that hole into the dark.

I remembered a can of tinned meat on the cabin shelf above the stove, so I spread some of that on a paper plate, put the plate outside the den entrance and waited. And waited some more.

Morning passed into afternoon. And I was thinking if the cat didn't want my offering I'd try some of it myself. But just then a small white face appeared in the opening.

"Come ahead," I said.

Hunger, I believe I've heard, is the second most powerful impulse after thirst. Or maybe it is third after something else. In any event, the white cat crept forward cautiously, sniffed what was on the plate, then forgot the threat of me entirely and fell to the feast.

And after eating, to my absolute astonishment, it came directly to me. It wasn't truly wild. Somewhere it had known a home, but then had gotten lost or been discarded. Its coat was matted, with leaves caught up in it. I could feel the creature trembling under my hand.

But then I gathered the little cat to me, carried it to the car, put it in a box, and it rode the two hours back to the city without uttering a sound.

We have a friend, a colleague of mine at the paper, who like us cares a great deal about cats. And my wife telephoned to offer him an opportunity.

"I can't do it," he said. "I already have too many cats. I just can't take another one."

There was a long silence on the line.

"What color is it?" he asked.

"It's white."

Another, shorter silence.

"OK," he said. "I'll take it."

The *it* turned out to be a *her*. And except for her growth having been held back by a spell on short rations, she was healthy.

We received regular reports of her blossoming and her accomplishments. She was much prized, and a future of affection was assured. *Happy* was the name our friend gave her, because she was happy to be found.

It was a great test of nerve to come out of the safety of the hole that autumn day and let herself be touched. But sometimes, if you're small and hungry, it can pay to take a chance.

65. TIP

THE BROOKLYN CAT arrived at Thanksgiving with the New York daughter, both traveling by plane at serious expense. Evidently she'd been a street creature, dodging cars and prowling through rubbish heaps — the cat, that is, not the daughter.

She wanted nothing to do with the other cats of the house, or with us. And she took immediate refuge in a cramped little niche in the side of a book table, roaring if approached too near. If you've spent any time in Brooklyn, you can see how a couple of years living wild in those ashcans and alleys might do that to you.

By Christmas, when the daughter came home for another visit, the recluse had begun to expand her range. There were reports of sightings in other parts of the house. But this was not what the military calls real-time intelligence. Because if you looked for her, always she was back in her lair, scowling out.

Then, in a moment of carelessness, the situation worsened.

Toward the last of the holidays we were about to set out on a short family trip. But where was the beast? Not in her hole. Not visible in any other room. Not in closets or under beds or even (for we looked) in drawers.

The basement door had been left ajar. *Could it be?*

we asked ourselves. *Surely not!* Then we descended into that dark and cluttered place, and of course that's where she'd gotten to. First onto a ledge at the top of the basement wall. Then onto a supporting beam. And finally, as we followed in hot pursuit, she'd darted through an opening into the crawl-space under an added room.

Cobwebs veiled the entrance to that awful cavity.

"OK," I declared. "That's it! I'm not going in there."

There was a moment's despairing silence, then the New York daughter spoke.

"I'll do it," she said. "I've been in there before." In childhood, with a small friend, she'd explored the ghastly underbelly of the house. At at age 10 or 11, she recalled it was.

So in she went — wriggling head-first through the opening, where quick things could be heard scuttling unseen in the darkness. Then she crept on hands and knees across the ancient dirt, through webs beaded with spiders' eggs and the husks of yesterday's arachnoid breakfasts.

And there, in fact, she did corner the fugitive and crawled back out a hero. And we got away together on our journey only four hours later than we'd meant to.

The daughters have left us now — gone back to their lives in Brooklyn and St. Louis. And I have resumed my courtship of the cat, whose name is Tip. Several times each day I go up to her room, taking bits of turkey on a saucer. For the first month she only glowered from her hole, and waited until I was gone to claim the treat.

Then she permitted me to step back and watch her eat, provided I made no advance. She's small, 4 pounds at most — a faintly marked gray tabby with white chin and vest, white feet, and white tip of tail.

It's two months that she's been with us, and just in the last week she has made great progress. She permits herself to be stroked, and even arches her back in visible pleasure. Sometimes, as I pass my hand lightly over her smooth coat, I'll feel her tremble suddenly and shrink away — perhaps overtaken by some memory of hurt. But that happens less often every day now, and passes sooner.

For any creature who's been so wounded by aloneness, it's not easy to learn to trust again.

Before many more weeks have gone by, I'm thinking she'll be out of her hole for good and finding her place with the others on our bed. Because it turns out the cat from Brooklyn really wasn't antisocial after all. Just untouched and unloved too long.

6 6 . M I C K E Y

THE *LITTLE* CAT WE CALL him. Or sometimes the *pink* one. Though he really is a pale orange tabby, who only looks pink in certain light. A foundling, like so many of us in this house, he joined our tribe after having failed under at least two other roofs. Even as a kitten, he had a survivor's toughness.

And he's fearless. He likes to trifle with the bird dogs while they eat. It is not recommended behavior. For Cyrus, breakfast is just another event in a crowded day. But Pete and Bear regard mealtime as an occasion of profound importance.

They look through the back door glass until they see me appear from the basement with their filled bowls. Then great joy overtakes them, and they do a kind of whirling dance until the door is opened.

The event always has been an electric one for the cats. The rattle of dry food going in the pans is the first alert. By the time the knob of the door to the back yard is turned, they have vanished into some other dimension.

All except orange Mickey. Hearing the food being portioned out, he comes from wherever he's been to wait for the dogs in the kitchen. He stands his ground, legs braced, directly in the pups' path as they shoulder past him. The can opener hums. The wet ration is mixed with the dry. The bowls are put down in a row — and Mickey makes his move.

It is comical and a little sad to see the two older hunting dogs, in all other ways brave creatures, bold and tireless in the field, undone by the prospect that a mite of a kitten might take their food.

Mickey advances to lie between them as they start to eat. Then he reaches out a paw to lightly touch Pete's nearest hind foot. The dog moves a bit to the side. The foot is touched again, provoking another retreat. Soon Pete is revolving around his food bowl like a planet around its sun.

It must amuse the little cat to find how slight an effort is required to set so large a beast in motion.

Sometimes he walks directly under the dog, causing Pete's chewing — possibly even his heart — to stop. Or he will shoulder close and press his cheek against the dog's, intending to share the ration.

Now Pete is roughly seven times the size of the cat by weight. It would never occur to me to try to take a steak off the plate of an 800-pound man. Or, if I did think of doing it, the impulse would be quickly overcome. Nor would I crawl under his chair and devil him around the ankles while he filled himself.

But finally, the pup just backs away in despair. He's hungry, but eating isn't worth the trouble and the risk. So Mickey has to be picked up and carried to another room, allowing the dog to be nourished in order that he may lead the way to quail when autumn comes.

Immediately, though, the cat is back, turning his attention now to Bear, who has a pricklier nature. Mickey moves forward one step at a time — just close enough to elicit a growl. Bear's tail is wagging, but the front end of him is making that unpleasant sound.

Causing the growl is the whole point, of course. It confirms that Mickey has achieved exactly that proximity which will produce the greatest possible anxiety, without provoking a charge. He lies down precisely there, watching the dogs wolf down whatever of their breakfast is left.

Bear used to be a finicky eater, dawdling over his food, sometimes looking first at his bowl, then up at me, resentful as some peasant faced with another year of nothing but potatoes and cabbage.

But now Bear doesn't loiter.

Unlike the other cats, Mickey is a plunger. I think I see in him the temperament of those people who wind up running corporations, taking the big chances, pulling down the big bonuses and the stock options, calling the tune for their hirelings to dance.

Though he's just five pounds now, he's most likely headed for something like 15 or 16. By then, I have no doubt, he'll have made himself master of this house and all who live in it. He'll eat when he wants and what he wants. The rest of us will just have to wait our turn.

Oddly, though, out of these dramas at the breakfast hour has come an understanding that, while not quite a friendship yet, is on the way to becoming one.

In the evenings, when food isn't the issue and all the various shapes and species of us are together in the bedroom — no great tension can be detected. Five-pound Mickey still can herd the pups around the room pretty much as he likes. If he decides to occupy a chair that one of them prefers to sleep in, there's no hope of reclaiming it.

The one who feels misused just whines piteously and finds another place.

But otherwise there's a fair amount of nose-touching and strategic sniffing. It will not be very long, I think, before we find two of them sharing a chair. That will not happen with the older, larger cats. *You're dogs,* their manner says. *We're a different family of creatures, and we're all better off just keeping our distance.*

But little Mickey seems not to put much stock in such distinctions. He's breaking new ground — crossing lines, making new friends, which always entails a bit of risk. And courage makes all the difference.

67 . AN ARMED TRUCE

THOUGH SHE'S BEEN relocated from her hole in the upstairs book table to the little back room just off the kitchen, Tip, the Brooklyn street cat, still mostly lives a life apart.

"She's very gentle. She likes being held." That was the Brooklyn daughter's description of her, by phone. But the progress of Tip's integration into the household has been, at best, uneven.

Remembering those words about her liking to be held, I tried to pick her up. The blood loss was not life-threatening, but it was untidy. Next time, if given a choice, I'd rather pet a live grenade, or hug a roll of concertina barbed wire.

Part of the problem, I believe, is that the other cats of the house have not been particularly cordial.

The orange tabby, Mickey, sits in the hall just outside the doorway, peering in. He's getting larger, and may appear to be a threat. But the truth is he's only mildly curious. Mickey can take cats or leave them. He doesn't think much about them, one way or the other. He prefers dogs.

Eric, the tuxedo cat, is full of years. The follies of youth are long behind him. It's the dark stillness of the basement he enjoys. He may not even have noticed there's a new beast among us.

Tommy, the gray one, is deeply insecure. And he compensates for that in the same way some children do, with swaggering and bluster. He glares with furious yellow eyes from the hallway into Tip's room. Sometimes he actually goes in there.

In the encounter that follows there are no injuries, but the jungle racket of it thunders through the house. And afterward, Tip regresses for a time, giving up whatever small progress she'd made toward sociability, refusing to let herself be touched.

Only the black cat, Scoop, is civil. And his friendliness is not without a certain self-interest. As a youngster he had the surgery that would relieve him of any future concern about family responsibilities. However, that small adventure at the clinic seems to have entirely slipped his mind. His devotion to Tip is therefore quite intense.

She will have surgery, too — when that is feasible. But in order to be loaded in a carrier and delivered to the veterinarian, she will have to be picked up. And at least for the moment, as I've indicated, trying that is absolutely out of the question.

I still have in my mind's eye the idyllic vision of Tip joining the rest of us on the bed, all of us nestled in a confusion of blankets and fur, pooling our warmth when the next ice storm brings down power lines and makes the house go cold.

That togetherness is nice to imagine, anyway, and you can count on me to let you know when it actually happens. But do not hold your breath.

68. DANGER AT DAWN

GREAT AGE HAS RENDERED Eric, the tuxedo cat, as fine and delicate as old china. His spirit is unbroken though. He still gives, and wants, affection. And he still is the peace-maker, the diplomat.

Through all the many comings and goings of others of his kind, he has been the one who welcomed them to the pride.

Tip has been the hardest case. Her previous life must have been a struggle. She trusted no one, had never felt a gentle hand. And she charged at Eric with a furious, hissing display.

He neither flinched nor retreated, but simply raised one forepaw as if in benediction, and fixed her with a level though uncombative stare, as if to say, *"Cut out the silliness. I have my place here, and you'll find yours. It will all work out."*

And it has. From that moment on there's been no trouble between them.

When Eric goes outdoors, it's only briefly and rarely much beyond the front porch step. In past years he would position himself under a bush, and his rabbit friend would approach. The two of them would consider one another from a distance of a few feet. Then the rabbit would go on his way, and Eric would call at the door to be let back in.

Now, when he returns from these brief adventures the other cats press close to him on either side as he makes his way to the kitchen and the food bowl.

In the dark of a recent morning, I heard through the open window beside the bed an unexpected sound: the *who who, who-whooo-aahh* of a barred owl proclaiming his territory somewhere in our city neighborhood. And when I went out to pick up the newspaper I heard the owl again. Then another. And a third — their calls overlapping, their three voices distinct.

Evidently Eric heard them, too, and stood motionless beside me on the walk, head inclined toward that strange and dangerous sound.

They're wonderful birds, barred owls. The literature says their wingspan can be as great as 40 inches. I love to hear them hooting, especially before daylight on a spring morning in the lowland woods when their calls start up a racket of turkeys gobbling.

Their preferred diet is mice, but they are reported to take prey as large as rabbits or even small foxes. So I picked Eric up and we went inside together.

He's hardly heavier than a rabbit now, and a good deal smaller than a fox. He'll miss his morning outings, though it will not be many more weeks before the weather turns nasty and uninviting.

And surely by the spring of his 19th year, the owls will have found a different place to hunt.

6 9 . SETTLING IN

AFTER A YEAR, I CAN stroke Tip almost at will. She once had owned the night pavements of Brooklyn — a gaunt and furtive shadow, ghosting between the pools of brightness under street lamps.

She is homeless no more. Nor is she gaunt. But neither is she wholly tame. For, as is true of children or any other creatures from hard beginnings, survivors do not give trust easily.

For months she trembled at the slightest touch, and sometimes lashed out in sudden terror. Now she likes being petted her whole length, from between her ears to the very end of her tail.

Immediately after the petting she always eats. This happens many times a day, and accounts for her dramatic change of shape. Once sinuous and agile, she has come more to resemble a rugby ball.

Another year or two and it might even be possible to pick her up, although I would not dream of trying it now unless there was a team of medics standing by with several units of whole blood.

That back room (Tip's room we call it) is where all the cats' bowls are kept, arranged there in a line. And she is touchy about her space.

Eric and Scoop come and go freely for nourishment. The others have to tread cautiously, trying to read her mood. The great mercy, from their perspective, is that she must sometimes sleep.

Little by little she is expanding her range.

One morning she came out from her room into the hall to watch the dogs take their breakfast. Evidently she'd seen dogs before, and did not seem much impressed.

Occasionally she ventures all the way into the kitchen when one of us is there, not to sit at our feet but reasonably nearby.

That's how she spends her days. It's her nights I wonder about.

At a certain time of evening, the pulse of our lives together slows. The dogs fold themselves onto bedroom chairs. Cats are arranged on the sofa, on radiator tops or with us in the bed. The house goes silent and dark.

The only illumination is a pool of brightness flung through the window from the street lamp at the curb. It is the hour when street cats are abroad, and when Tip is a Brooklyn cat again.

It pleases me to think that while the rest of us are lost in dreaming, she owns the house, finding its secret places, measuring the corners with her whiskers, moving freely and unfrightened in the dark.

And while there must surely have been adventure in that former life, I like to imagine she understands in some primal way the luck of having been found, and kept, and touched — even if she has to let those others share her room by day.

70. LOVE AT 100

ERIC IS IN HIS 19TH YEAR — somewhere around 100 in cat years. But great age has not dulled his passion. During the recent sharp spell of early autumn weather, he fell deeply, ungovernably in love.

With the furnace.

In youth, he was plump and sleek as an otter. Now, when stroking him, you can feel his architecture through the skin. And he's gone nearly deaf. He's like those people who, having lost their hearing in their latter years, conduct conversations in a shout. What he imagines is a simple mew — signaling his desire for a treat or for attention — comes out a hoarse bleat.

He's not at all feeble, still able to make it unaided onto the bed at night, though his getting there is not pretty to watch. And because the seniors of any species tend to feel the cold most acutely, it's my wife's side he prefers, the side with the electric blanket set on high.

In the morning, if in his opinion the sleepers have languished abed too long, he brings his face close to theirs and, as he's done from the very first, whiskers them awake.

It's in the daytime that Eric heads directly for the basement.

I've written about our furnace before. The cast-iron boiler is roughly the size of a compact car. It is 82 years old, the original equipment, and, like Eric, may very well be immortal.

Every morning now our routine is the same.

I have heated my cereal in the microwave and carried my bowl to the table. Upstairs, the electric blanket has been switched off and the bed is being made.

Just as I am sitting to eat, Eric strides into the breakfast room wearing an expression of urgent purpose, stands facing the basement door and emits his horrific yowl.

"All right," I tell him. "Go for it!"

I open the door and he plunges down the dark stairway, hellbent for comfort. And that's where he spends his day, cozied up against the iron boiler as if it were the great mother of all cats.

Hours later, some errand may take one of us to the basement. Sometimes Eric will bestir himself, and walk over to be acknowledged. More often, though, he will be all but invisible lying far back in the furnace's shadow, and you will see him peering out with inexpressible satisfaction.

It occasionally happens that we forget to call him up in the evening. It's not a crisis, because my wife has put auxiliary bowls of food and water down there, positioned nearby for his convenience.

The next day, when he does finally emerge, his black coat is gray with basement dust. And he is almost too hot to touch.

There've been dogs in my life that I've been awfully fond of. And there was a 1947 Chevrolet I liked a lot. But except for my wife, daughters and other immediate family, I don't believe I've ever cared for anything in this world with quite the same abject devotion Eric feels for his furnace.

But Eric doesn't drive, and doesn't keep dogs, and doesn't have a wife or daughters. And the electric blanket is an on-again, off-again thing.

You just make do with what you have.

71 . HOPE OF MAGIC

THE PINK CAT, MICKEY, likes to spend part of each day here on the enclosed side porch where I work, surrounded by books and seashells and stacks of paper and my wife's flowering plants.

In fact he prefers to be with us wherever we are, a trait more doglike than catlike. He follows in the house wherever we go, and cannot bear to be alone.

He is easy company — easier than can be found in a lot of the places where writers tend to hang out.

Mickey does not chatter away inconsiderately while one is trying to think. He does not whistle or tap a pencil on the desk top or have any other of the annoying habits that are so common among professional scribblers.

He is, in fact, a perfect gentleman, respectful of another's space and need to concentrate.

The door to the porch has glass panes top to bottom. He studies me through one of the lower panes, likely trying to determine what sort of mood I'm in. If the moment seems propitious, he knocks, and I admit him.

He strides in quietly, and with much dignity — although not at all puffed up with his own importance. He simply is glad to be part of this enterprise, whatever the enterprise is.

Sometimes there is a bird in the bush outside the porch window. Or a fat squirrel on a lower branch of the pine at the corner of the house. Mickey's jaws work furiously and would make a chittering sound — except that he is careful not to let the teeth come quite together.

For the most part, though, he just sits and contemplates the outside world.

Yesterday, he chose a place on the window ledge, where the sun fell warmly through the glass. But after a while the sun's position changed, and that spot no longer suited him. So Mickey moved to the couch, whose pillows are covered by a sheet to prevent the color from fading in direct light. He worked his way under the sheet and curled there, nicely snugged in.

As spectator activities go, watching someone in the act of writing must be about on a par with watching grass grow. When the novelty wears off, he comes over to press against my leg, then stretches, and stands patiently facing the door. It has occurred to him the other cats may have found more electric amusements.

So I let him out, and sort around in my bag of words, hunting for another paragraph or two.

Before long, though, he's back, rapping again with his paws on the glass of the door. And I am pleased to see him, because mine is a solitary occupation. A congenial presence — so long as it's a reasonably quiet one — is welcome.

My fine old bird dog, Rufus, used to keep me company while I worked. He slept on the wicker couch, yelping just a little in his dreams. We were indifferent to time, then, he and I. The years and the seasons passed unnoticed while I sat here, typing. And time took Rufus away, as it takes us all.

Mickey is a youngster, though. Nothing about him speaks of endings yet. He's an immensely optimistic creature, for one so small, and his spirit lets me imagine myself young, too.

Each time, he comes in here full of hope that there'll be something more interesting than the deliberate *clickety-clicking* of my writing machine. Maybe this time, he thinks, there'll be a little magic in that room.

Sometimes I dare to let myself hope that, too. And once in a great while, if only briefly, there is.

72. HE IS SUNLIGHT

DOGS AND CATS, IN myth at least, are a famously uneasy mix. But besides the 25 cats, we've shared our house with eight dogs, all but one of them sturdy hunting dogs. That's more than 30 furred lodgers in all. And though there've been transient misunderstandings, we've never had a war.

Besides the residents, we've known others — ones passing through, or ones we met on our way to somewhere.

There was a fine big tabby that woke us with its mewing outside the motel door in Goodland, Kansas, where we stopped one winter night driving home from Colorado.

We will remember always the tiny kitten that came to us out of the vast *taiga*, the forest of eastern Siberia, to nestle between our sleeping bags, and the sadness we felt at having to leave that little creature behind.

The good part is the friendship and sometimes the comfort these creatures have given to us and often to each other. The hard part has been the losses, of which we've lately had another — the one we called Headlight because of the way his eyes shone out of the darkness of his face.

But long before the grieving, there's all the joy. And on those darker days, orange Mickey supplies the needed sunlight. The very sight of him is cheering. He is not as verbal as Oliver was, and as some others have been. But he is clearly communicating. When spoken to — and we speak to him a lot — he opens his mouth in a silent but perfectly congenial reply.

He used to be *little* Mickey. The adjective became a habit, and seemed a proper prefix to his name. But he's a small cat no longer. At the last weighing, he was a husky 14 pounds. He has a tiger's markings, though his are paler. And he is civil with the other cats, even if it's the company of dogs that he prefers.

When the Brittanys come in at night, he races up the stairs after them. He and Cyrus tussle good-naturedly a bit. Pete and Bear greet him with a touch of noses. Then Mickey settles down to watch some television.

At the evening's end, when the lights go out, he

claims his regular place between us on the bed. The plump warmness of him can be sensed there in the dark. And he still is there when the clock-radio, at 6:20 each the morning, begins to speak the day's first news.

I throw back the covers and hurry downstairs to fill the dogs' pans, and Mickey goes with me, stropping himself against my leg as I open the cans and mix the food. He has lost his power to devil the pups while they eat.

In fact, he sometimes presses his cheek against Pete's or Bear's when they're at their bowls. Pete doesn't dance away and Bear does not emit even the smallest growl. They know very well now that he's a friend — one of them, one of us all.

When I go to fetch the morning newspapers from the front walk, Mickey follows me to the door. And if I'm inattentive for just a moment, he will fly past me and out. He really wouldn't dream of going anywhere. For immediately then he rolls over on the brick walk and, entirely satisfied, waits to be carried back inside. He only does it to prove he can.

It's in that same spirit he makes a point several times a day of visiting the lair of Tip, the Brooklyn beauty who's warmed to humans but still has not much use for others of her kind. With a fine show of bravado, he simply strolls in that back room, has a bite or two of food — though there are other rations available in the kitchen.

Then he bounds up to a window sill, sniffs the world beyond the screen. And when he's satisfactorily made his point, he saunters out again without so much as glancing at the owner of that space.

It would be impossible to rank these many cats according to the happiness they've brought us. We've never even tried. I will say this of Mickey, though: In much the same way that the first one, Oliver, gave me to understand what wonders cats could be, Mickey by his grace of spirit somehow summarizes the virtues of all those that have followed.

He has been one of the great gifts of our later lives. It is impossible to imagine our private world without him. And to be honest, I'd rather not even try.

ENDINGS

73. THE HOUSE LION

When he was new in this world, and had no wisdom, a blown leaf in the park was his mortal enemy.

For the first six years he had one apartment window of sun. And waited warm on the sill through the silent afternoons of his mistress's working bachelorhood. The darting birds, too, alarmed him.

The second six years he prowled the larger kingdom of a house — shared it with a heavy-footed man, the man's three dogs, two creeping infants in their time. Survived the barkings-at and the intemperate huggings. Dispensed justice with a paw whose claws he kept sheathed. Mastered them all.

Caught a basement mouse, once. Brought it up in the morning to display. Then, not knowing how to kill it — or maybe why to kill it — let it get away. His one trophy.

Grew old, more patient. Let dogs and children touch noses with him. Slept a lot.

Watched the new cat come, a shaggy fugitive from the homeless cold of winter — and must have read in that the first sign of things ending, others beginning. But made his peace yet again. Slipped away one whole night with that new cat, that outdoor cat. Saw things he'd never dreamed of, and came back smelling of the jungle, eyes narrowed to slits of ancient triumph.

Moved slower now. Slept more. Remembered it all — the leaf, the darting birds, his mouse, that stolen night. Was full of years.

Lay down at last on a friendly rug.

Did not wake up.

Still prowls sometimes, at the eye's corner, in a certain fall of sunlight in an empty room.

ANOTHER CAT AT THE DOOR
was designed by Gene Funk, David Spaw and Sharon Hanson,
digitally composed in Adobe Weiss
and printed on Weyerhauser's Natural Cougar Opaque,
a neutral pH paper with an expected 300-year library
storage life as determined by the Council of Library Resources
of the American Library Association,
by
Greystone Graphics, Inc.
Kansas City, Kansas 66103
USA